Thinking OUTSIDE THE BOX

on Race, Faith and Life

Bishop Dr Joe Aldred

Published by Hansib Publications, 2013

Hansib Publications Limited
P.O. Box 226, Hertford, Hertfordshire, SG14 3WY
United Kingdom

www.hansibpublications.com

ISBN 978-1-906190-65-1

A CIP catalogue record for this book
is available from the British Library

Printed in Great Britain

To my late mother Iona Caroline Aldred, who taught me by example how to think for myself

Thanks to God – Creator and Sustainer. To my immediate and extended family, friends and all those who challenge and stimulate my mind: thank you. Special mention to my long-suffering wife Novelette, my sister Winsome who read and tweaked the manuscript, and to everyone at Hansib Publications for their dedication to seeing this project through to publication.

CONTENTS

INTRODUCTION

This volume is a collection of homilies, talks, lectures, sermons, presentations and articles. They are of varying lengths, styles and contents as bespeaks the different settings in which they first emerged. Inevitably there are overlapping themes and repeats, even some occasions where the same topic is treated quite differently, but I have decided to leave them all in nonetheless. The reader can, if the reader wishes, read sequentially chapter by chapter but this book is not meant to be read this way. Rather, I advise a look at the index so that you can locate the chapter/s that appeal to you at any given time.

Some tweaking has been done for readability and in response to feedback to the originals. Together, this eclectic mix of in-your-face reflections represents aspects of my mixed-portfolio life as a bishop without portfolio, ecumenist, broadcaster, speaker and writer in Britain. Be challenged, but enjoy!

Part 1

RACE

CHAPTER 1

Black I certainly am

I believe all humanity is made in the image and likeness of God the Creator and therefore is intrinsically worthy of the highest regard. In my cosmology woe betides, in this life or the next, anyone who dehumanises another human being – God will hold them to account at the judgement! But I am wondering if it is possible that by our response to racist abuse we sometimes inadvertently hand power over to the racist. I cannot guarantee that others will accord me the appropriate level of human regard, but my response is in my power alone. For example, I refuse to allow anyone to hurt me by name-calling. My sense of selfhood is such that name-calling, with or without expletives intended to cause hurt, does not hurt me. However, that does not prevent me invoking the law if I think someone has broken it, not least because it is clear that racists must be stopped since not every race-hate victim is able to so resist them psychologically, emotionally or spiritually.

My reflection on this subject arises from the hullabaloo over racist taunts directed at Formula One racing driver Lewis Hamilton in Barcelona in 2011, in an apparent attempt to disrespect Hamilton's humanity as a person of mixed racial heritage. I know little of Hamilton's response to the incident, more about the public outcry over it. I am cognisant of what the press' interests are in running the story – the press seeks to attract more readers, listeners and viewers – but I am less clear about the mindset and response of my fellow Blacks to the story of White Barcelonans blacking up as a means of taunting Hamilton. I am driven to ponder what is going on in the psyche of Black people in Britain concerning skin colour. We already know what is going on in the minds of White racists, if we can credit them with thinking – they believe that Whiteness puts them at the top of the pyramid of human development and civilisation. But I am now questioning whether some Black people's hypersensitive response to racist White people's attitude and behaviour towards the colour of our skin belies an unpalatable truth: that some Black people actually have imbibed the White racist inspired propaganda that there is something innately wrong with being Black.

One Spanish press headline bleared out, "Lewis Hamilton endures racist taunts from spectators at Formula 1 testing".[1] So what happened? A group of White young people wore wigs, dark makeup and T-shirts with the words 'Hamilton's family' written on them. I would never wish to make light of racism, however, is it not the truth that so long as we all, Black and White, regard being called Black as an insult, White racists will have a trump card they can play against Black people and win at will? And if you had a dead-cert winning hand, wouldn't you play it, and often? Of course you would. Currently, the most inarticulate and absurd White person can immobilise the most articulate Black person by simply referring to his/her skin colour in an implied or explicitly derogative manner and it's game, set and match to the White dumb inarticulate. Why should I give anyone such power over me?

Over the years we have seen a massive drive to eliminate racism from sport, bolstered by anti-racism laws in Britain. Still, racist taunts continue, as does racism in multitudinous forms in sports and society at large. In some other parts of Europe with less legal protection, racists have a field day at the expense of people of darker hue. If we think that one day it will all end – forget it! At least, not voluntarily on the part of White bigots. Why should they give up on such an easy gig? If you find an opponent's Achilles heel would you voluntarily practice abstinence? I don't think so. I am restricting reference here to racism at a popular social level since I am clear that some forms of racism are structural. We should spare nothing to systematically and determinedly tear down racist structures – wrestling against principalities and powers and spiritual wickedness in high places – and note that although some White people do not engage personally in racist behaviour, they are still part of a society where racism persists structurally to the detriment of people of colour.

Yet I am convinced that if racism is to be eradicated, which I seriously doubt will ever happen on this side of eternity, Black and White people must collaborate to dismantle racist structures and reorientate behaviour. The biggest change however, in my personal view, lays with a change in Black people's attitude to the blackening up, monkey chants, banana waving and name calling directed at us. But how? Top of my list is that we need to get to a place where someone calling a Black person Black is made to sound and look what they are, ridiculous, because that is precisely what I am, Black! Yes, Whites must own up to institutional racism endemic in the fabric of British society and its pillars that were not designed with the interests of Black people in mind. The powers that be must change the laws and regulations that support institutional racism. But at a popular cultural level Black people must embrace their Black humanity and cease to overact to name-calling. A kind of response that says, "who are you calling Black?" immediately problematises being Black.

Too many of us apparently do not embrace the Black self, as may be evident by us being deeply hurt and upset by being called Black. In too many Black minds, so it seems, being Black is a problem some appear to be willing to do all in their power to mitigate or neutralise. Evidently, for some, being born Black is a problem, a curse even. I am intrigued by the way many Black sportspeople and celebrities, for example, appear blind to Blackness in their choice of social spaces and partners. That some never seem to see another Black person as a potential partner suggests to me that these Black people may be in denial about their Black humanity, or if they do own their Black self, they are rather embarrassed by it and do everything in their power to compensate by assimilating into White society. When a Black person is not accepting of him/herself because to them Black conjures up undesirable ugliness, if someone calls them Black, of course they will be offended! The White racist has therefore an endless supply of raw material of Black self-denying negativity towards the Black self because, "can the Ethiopian change his skin?" (Jeremiah 13.23). No more than a leopard its spots. Unless, that is, skin-whitening cream is brought into the equation. Black people need to embrace the Garveyite doctrine of Black self-love and never be embarrassed by our God-given colour and ethnicity, or as Garvey would call it, our race. This is echoed in the biblical words of the Songs of Solomon, "I am Black and beautiful" (not Black 'but' beautiful as the King James Version of the Bible chose to render it).

The battle over racism is never going to be won in the court houses of this world (necessary as court action may be when people break the law); it will be won in the minds of people. Black people must be the first to win this battle and we will when psychologically we alight upon a place of inner self-belief and self-love based upon self-acceptance, where no one succeeds in offending us by calling us Black, darkening White faces, wearing dreadlocks wigs, scratching their armpits or throwing bananas. Of course, when they break the law let us ensure they feel its full force, but not because their words or actions have seared our innermost selves like a hot iron. This is not so much a legal as an ideological and psychological battle; when being Black ceases to be a problem to Black people, it will soon cease to be a tool used by Whites to offend Blacks. To the Black person such taunts will attract a response akin to swatting flies, irritants but incapable of scarring our souls. After all, if you make monkey noises and scratch your armpits like a monkey, maybe you are the monkey. Of course not everybody is strong enough to respond in this way and the vulnerable are to be defended and supported, including taking legal action against violators of our humanity where appropriate.

So, go ahead, call me Black because that is precisely who and what I am; an African, Black, beautifully and wonderfully made in the image and likeness of the Creator!

Note: A version of this first appeared as an article in the Vive Magazine online

1. http://www.thespainforum.com/f188/autos-lewis-hamilton-endures-racist-taunts-spain-83560/

CHAPTER 2

Faith and race

I am greatly honoured to be asked to present a perspective on 'Faith and Race' as part of the scene setting of this important conference. Let me thank the West Midlands Faiths Forum, the genesis of which I had a small hand in, for bringing us together around the theme of 'Light and Shade'. This is an intriguing topic, and one that I hope will provoke deep thought leading to action at this important moment in our development together here in Birmingham, in our country, in Europe and indeed in the wider world – I'm probably being a little over-ambitious.

It is now a cliché to say that we live in a multi-faith and multi-cultural society. But of course it is true. Here in Birmingham we pride ourselves on our reputation as one of the most diverse cities in Britain. In our city we find traditional Christianity, Islam, Sikhism, Hinduism, Judaism, Buddhism, Rastafarianism, Humanism and several other expressions of faiths and beliefs. We know also that within most if not all of these faiths and beliefs are internal denominations. As Brian Davies reminds us, religious beliefs are many and varied.[1] Birmingham is as diverse as anywhere on the planet in terms of human identity and religious following.

I cannot however go on without picking a fight with the term 'race'. A strong case can be made for rejecting the term race just as we have rejected 'Negro', because of its historical pseudo-scientific reasoning, or its 'genomic construction' as Paul Gilroy calls it.[2] Gilroy goes on to say that the pursuit of liberation from 'race' is an especially urgent matter for the peoples who, like modern Blacks in the period after the transatlantic slavery, were assigned an inferior position in the enduring hierarchies that raciology creates. So may I put in a plug for the idea that if we must use the term 'race', let's use it in the context that there is only one race – the human race, and therefore not pay homage to the spurious, divisive and damaging categorisation of humanity that race represents.

After my little tantrum about 'race', for which I will substitute 'ethnicity' from here on, let me go on to reiterate that Birmingham is rich in its ethnic mix based upon the many nationalities and cultures that co-exist here. The 2001 Census serves us up a rich blend of Caucasians, Asians, Africans, Caribbeans, Chinese, mixed heritages and more. In recent times new migrations and changing demographics have meant that the ethnic landscape has become increasingly complex. What is happening in Birmingham is microcosmic of the further diffusion of human homogeneity that is accruing across the world according to Yasmin Alibhai-Brown.[3] We could argue over whether we are moving towards or away from homogeneity, even whether it has ever existed, but in places like Birmingham what is undeniable is that we are living in increasingly closer proximity, even if living along parallel lines, whilst simultaneously increasing in diversity. It seems to me that whether the purists and essentialists like it or not, we are moving both closer together and further apart at the same time. Speaking as a person of Caribbean heritage, nowhere has this become truer than in the Caribbean, typified by Jamaica's national motto, 'Out of many one people'.

Where does this brief sketch of the cocktail of ethnicity and faith leave us? Well, let me suggest that we are in a very difficult situation indeed concerning identities, not least because although most of us are very particular about our own identity, we are essentially intellectually lazy when it comes to the identities of others. We seem to like nothing better than a little game of finding easy catch-all boxes, pigeonholes and stereotypes to put people in. Too many distinctions and different ethnicities, different cultures, different heritages, different faiths and different denominations within faiths wear us out. So we prefer to resort to broad terms such as Asians or Muslims, and of course they all own corner shops. Black people are Pentecostals or Rastafarians, gang members or yardies or lazy. And of course, all White people are Christians; in fact they are all Anglicans, Roman Catholics or Methodists. We generally can't be bothered, have not got the patience for the particularities of individuality or small group distinctions. Stopping to find out about the one is too time-consuming in an age of fast food automated consumerism.

As I have hinted above, ours is a hugely multifaceted and super complex situation. A survey of the 2001 Census shows that people of

Caribbean heritage have a belonging to some degree in all categories of faith cited in the Census. We belong to every Christian denomination and every other faith group in this country. This means that the similarities and differences between ethnicity and faith demand attention and analysis, not simplistic assumptions. We learn very quickly that no one ethnic type can lay claim to any one faith, and vice versa. I have even met some White Rastas! Bhikhu Parekh reminds us that however rich it might be, no culture embodies all that is valuable in human life or develops the full range of human possibilities. Different cultures, he argues, thus correct and compliment each other, expand each other's horizon of thought and alert each other to new forms of human fulfilment.[4] An inquisitive attitude is helpful in such contexts.

Much has been made of the term 'respect' in recent times. The government is, as we meet, developing a respect agenda to assist and energise their community cohesion agenda. I believe that a good place to start is with the understanding of 'respect' that I favour. It means to 'look again' as in the Latin *respecio*, i.e. 're' (back) 'specio' (to look, to see). To respect is to look back or again, to become familiar with. If we can expunge intellectual laziness from our culture and replace it with the imperative of knowing, then I believe we will achieve something quite astonishing. Imagine what would happen if we all knew each other really well, our different histories, aspirations, likes and dislikes. Imagine, were we to make every racist, particularly those found guilty of such a crime, study history, including Black history and culture! They would soon find out, for example, that Africa had civilisations long before the Europeans enslaved millions of us, turned us into chattel and attempted to make us subhuman. We can throw stones only at objects at a distance from us, we can't punch the person we are hugging close, and we tend to be discriminatory towards those we don't know, don't like or care for. The answer is to respect others.

I suggest that a sound premise on which we can move forward in terms of ethnicity and faith is that of making a point of truly knowing ourselves, our true history and contemporary reality, our hopes for the future. And then as we do that to ourselves, so we do to others. Get to know the other's true history, contemporary reality, and the other's hope for the future. If we apply this principle to our humanity and our faith then I believe we have a bright future as West Midlanders together in our lovely yet challenging multi-cultural, multi-ethnic and multi-faith area. May we truly be able to say that out of many we are one people. Thank you.

From an address to the West Midlands Faiths Forum

1. Brian Davies (ed) Philosophy of Religion, p2
2. Paul Gilroy, Against Race, p15
3. Yasmin Alibhai-Brown, Who do we think we are?, p28
4. Bhikhu Parekh, Rethinking Multiculturalism, p167

CHAPTER 3

Race and progress

This summer, my wife and I holidayed in south Florida. The sunshine and warm weather were as welcomed as was the opportunity to visit both our extended families. In addition to this being a family holiday, I did a little mousing around. My wife's sister assists the Mayor of a new three-year-old city called Miami Gardens and on a visit to their administrative offices, I discovered some fascinating information. Miami Gardens is a Black-majority city, 70% of its 107,000 population are Black (i.e. African American, Black Caribbean and Africans), 16% Hispanics and 3% White, plus other ethnic groups. Seven of the city's eight top officials – the elected mayor and six councillors – are Black! Only the city manager is White and of course I could not help noticing the absence of Hispanics in the leadership team, in spite of their significant 16% presence in the make up of the small city's population. Whist this leadership profile seemed on the surface highly empowering for Blacks, I kept wondering whatever happened to diversity. Why and where had all the White people gone from this little part of America? In conversation, the Mayor indicated that there were some Blacks who were unhappy about having a White city manager, preferring an all Black local government.

I was interested too to note that a recent US Census Bureau report indicated that 30%, or 100 million, of the 300 million US population are from minority ethic backgrounds, with people of Caribbean heritage making up 0.8% or 2.4 million of the national population. Florida has a population of 18 million people, 39%, or 7 million, of which are ethnic minorities, of which 17%, or 1.2 million, are of Caribbean heritage. I discovered that within this ethnic mix were many of the same ills we are accustomed to in Britain. The Mayor spoke of educational underachievement, social deprivation, poverty, shootings, and various forms of alienation and exclusion of some individuals and groups from wider society. As in the UK, these conditions exist cheek by jowl with the affluence of a privileged few. I reflected upon the universality of these issues and was reminded of the biblical truisms that there is nothing new under the sun, and the poor you have with you always. I was assured that the city officials were doing all in their power to address these matters, but it was all taking time.

I was told that Jamaicans do well in Florida. So it was no surprise when during our visit news broke that a 23-year-old Jamaican-born African American, Barrington Irving, had become the youngest person to fly solo around the world. He landed at Opa-locka Executive Airport near Miami after a three-month journey (clearly not a direct flight!) in an airplane he had built with $300,000 sponsorship money. The lengthy prayer meeting that took place on the airport tarmac in the full gaze of the waiting press was an apt reminder that Irving's was a Christian family and that he was supported by a community of faith – so important for Black people the world over. It was hoped that his feat would inspire interest in aviation and encourage other African Americans to think outside the box of basketball, rapping and acting. I couldn't help but wonder why Jamaicans in Florida and the USA in general appear to be among the highest achievers, in contrast to the situation in Britain. Why is it that Caribbean migrants have held on to their faith in Britain, but not the entrepreneurial instincts that brought them here?

For whatever reason even into the third and fourth generations since the Windrush, Caribbean people have yet to impress themselves significantly on the socio-political and economic life of Britain. Could it be that the low social status of the majority of Jamaican economic migrants who came to Britain in the Windrush era remains a key factor, lending itself more to religion – Karl Marx's opiate of the people – than to economics and politics? If so, then as Jamaicans and other Caribbean-heritage people in Britain become more socially, economically and politically upwardly mobile, we may expect a greater level of achievement all round. The chicken and egg paradox comes to mind. Which came first? If Caribbean people in Britain are to excel, education and the nature of the education process will play a major role.

I was also much exercised learning about a ruling by the US Supreme Court, by a 5:4 majority, to reject 'race' as a factor in deciding the composition of schools in the USA's education system, as they tried to stem the growing tide of segregation that appeared to be worryingly resurgent since the 1990s. In attempting to ensure racially integrated schools, authorities in Louisville and Seattle had adopted a policy of quotas that included bussing in pupils to ensure the racial quotas were maintained. This attempt at social engineering was thought by some to resemble the discredited and discarded 'separate but equal' doctrine that was outlawed in 1954 by the Supreme Court. The Justices now decided that the notion of diversity should not be focused on a student's race. One of the Justices said he believed racial determinants "may entrench the very prejudices we seek to overcome".

Again I could not help but reflect upon our own struggles in Britain and our attempts to raise the educational attainment of Black boys in particular. Strategic separation has been proposed, with separate classes for Black boys, entire Black schools even, based on the Black-led church model that appears to have been a success in Britain leading to the empowerment for many Black Christians. Is America leading the way here in rejecting race as an instrument of integration in schools? Or are the Justices being naive in thinking that as significant a factor as race or ethnicity can be excluded in the discourse and policy-making around integration and cohesion? Furthermore, does an emphasis on race necessarily promote attitudes of racial inferiority and superiority? Can we not discern between racial profiling for good aimed at inclusion as opposed to exclusion as existed under apartheid in South Africa and Jim Crow laws in the USA?

There are no simple answers to the array of complex issues that confront us locally and globally. As the Black Mayor and colleagues of Miami Gardens and record-breaking pilot Barrington Irving, along with a host of others, among them Colin Powell, show, like any other people given the right motivation and support anyone, Jamaicans included, can achieve their potential. But if we are to achieve the dream of Dr Martin Luther King, that one day we will live in a world in which our worth is not judged by the colour of our skins but the content of our characters, then a serious dilemma faces us in Britain. How much longer can we measure progress by colour whilst simultaneously maintaining that colour does not or should not matter? Nowhere is this dilemma more glaring than in the Christian church, which espouses that all are made equal in the image of the one Creator God and belong to the one catholic church. Yet, as someone has observed, 11 o'clock on Sunday mornings is the church's most divided hour as worshipping 'birds of a feather' flock together according to ethnic, cultural, national and denominational allegiances. The apostle Paul insists that Christ has broken down the wall of division between people, thereby creating one out of many, and "there is neither Jew or Gentile, bond or free, male or female" (Galatians 3.28). This is really deep because I have been a Christian for a long time yet the last time I checked I was still male! I cannot quite work out whether or not race must be de-emphasised in the interest of progress or whether indeed in a racialised world race pride and ethnic identity are drivers for progress. I lean instinctively toward the latter, but I feel another holiday in the sun coming on.

First published in The Vine Magazine, 2008

CHAPTER 4

Racism awareness

INTRODUCTION

Racism attacks the very core, the essence of our common humanity; it should not be practiced or tolerated in the church. Indeed, in this regard the church ought to be an example to the rest of society. I, at least, hold to the view that to 'defeat' racism, we must understand it: what it is, where it comes from and what sustains it. So before addressing what I believe we need to do to 'defeat' racism in the church and society, I want to address myself to these prior matters.

WHAT IS RACISM?

There are so many 'isms' in the world that it is very easy for racism to be, covertly if not overtly, dismissed as another annoying politically correct 'ism'. So allow me to, in the words of former Prime Minister John Major, but hopefully without succumbing to his fate, get back to basics by offering an answer to the fundamental question, 'What is racism?' I begin by citing the 1976 Race Relations Act. This Act of Parliament made it illegal for a person to discriminate against another on racial grounds. According to that Act, to discriminate means to treat less favourably, or to apply other requirements or conditions than would normally be applied. On 'racial grounds' refer to discrimination due to a person or group's colour, race, nationality or ethnic or national origins. So, we could say, racism means to treat someone less favourably on account of their colour, race, nationality, ethnic or national origins. It is worthy of note too that 'race' is a compound term; it does not mean any one thing and it is a naturally fluid, dynamic feature of humanity.

Two further points can be usefully made here. First, what applies to the individual is applicable also to groups of people. Second, sometimes treating individuals or groups less favourably because of their colour, race, et al. can be perpetrated not only by individuals, but also by systems and institutions as well. As with individuals, systems and institutions may not always be "conscious, wilful or deliberate" in perpetrating racism. However, as the Stephen Lawrence Inquiry found, "a White-dominated organisation is liable to have procedures, practices and a culture which tend to exclude or disadvantage non-White people."[1] "Unwitting racism" it was called. Subsequent to the Lawrence Inquiry, the Race Relations (Amendment) Act 2000 extended the 1976 Act by placing a duty on public bodies to promote race equality. With this, 'racism awareness' has become entrenched in our culture, and the industry in anti-racism training, for example, has flourished.

As Christians, it is worth trying to understand racism from a biblical and theological perspective also. Whilst in the past the Bible and theological propositions have been used to support racism – most notably during the Transatlantic Slave Trade and more recently in South Africa – the primordial position of the Bible is, I argue, anti-racist. Genesis 1.27 says, "So God created man in His own image; in the image of God He created him; male and female He created them". Genesis 2.7 says, "And the Lord God formed man of the dust of the ground, and breathed into his nostrils the breath of life; and man became a living being". I deduce from this that humanity has the same beginning, is of the one divine image, come from the same mother earth, and is of the one God-breathed existence. In support of this I cite Paul speaking at the Areopagus in Athens about "God who made the world and everything in it – 'the whole race of men'[2] – from one blood" (Acts 17.24&26). People of faith, and Christians in particular, do well to embrace the Latin slogan 'Imago Dei' as a way of expressing the idea of humanity made in the image of God. And as Alistair McGrath suggests, "the fact that humanity is created in the image of God is widely regarded as establishing the original uprightness and dignity of human nature".[3] Whatever convenient deviations there have been from this central truth, let us agree at least that originally all of us are of one stock, and that one stock is the essence of the divine. The acceptance that every human being is stamped 'Imago Dei' is a good place to begin our relationships with each other.

WHERE IT COMES FROM

But just how did we get to where we are – a racialised world in which 'race' signals "immutable divisions of humankind" each biologically, intellectually and linguistically homogeneous, and in which, as the Americans say, "If you're Black, step back; if you're brown, stick around, if you're White you're alright"? We may be gradually moving away from some of the rigidity of this model, but it is still a controlling factor over our lives especially here in the western world. This is why we note moments like the first African American to become president of the US, the first Black member of the British Cabinet, the first Black football manager in the Premiership, et al.

One writer who has helped my understanding is Ivan Hannaford. He argues that 'race' as an organising principle is a strictly western idea, a product of the Enlightenment.[4] Hannaford suggests that from ancient times until the fifth century and Augustine's reconciliation of faith and politics, the major divisions between people were between the civic and the barbarous, i.e. civilised and uncivilised. He further suggests that from then to the Reformation, the Greco-Roman organising concept was based on blood relationship expressed through family, tribe and clan. Hannaford then argues that post-reformation, arcane threads of racial accounts of human existence were extracted from early Chaldean, Hermetic and Cabalist writings alluding to blood, physiognomy, climate, land, soil and language. This, he suggests, was the prelude to three distinct phases of the development of a conscious idea of race in the west. I have neither the time nor expertise to unpack Hannaford's thesis, but a brief mention of the three phases is needed.

1684-1815: 'RACE' AS ETHNIC GROUPS

According to Hannaford, between the expulsion of the Jews and Moors from Spain and the landing of the first Negro in the North American colonies in 1619, the word 'race' entered Western Languages.[5] Originally it denoted mathematical or astrological lines, or being of good, noble or pure lineage – primarily with reference to the order of kings and bishops i.e. good Christian people as opposed to barbarous infidels – but this gradually gave way to race as a signifier of physical and cultural differentiation between Europeans and the people they were encountering on their voyages of discovery. Initially the European intent was to make civility of these heathens by conversion to Roman Catholicism, by force if necessary, and there were various papal bulls to that effect. However, European expansionism required the enslavement and/or colonisation of these heathens – Africans and Indians, and so it became expedient that these were not just heathens to be converted, but inferior species against which any necessary cruelty in the subjugation process was justified.

To embed inferiority, various pseudoscientific theories were advanced about brain size, skull thickness, laziness, etc. Theological pronouncements justified conquests in the interest of saving the souls of the heathen. Aristotle's conclusion that some men, though human, may be by nature slaves, confirmed the inferiority of Indians and Africans, people of darker hue, as an inferior ethnos to the White European conquerors. Against this background, the colonisation of North America was marked by prejudice, discrimination and race hatred.[6] The dynamic Germanic peoples were thought to possess personal quality, or genius, that flowed through their bloodline but was absent from their Indian and African subjects who were qualitatively different, inferior. Towards the end of the 18th century, anthropologist Johann Friedrich Blumenbach (1752-1840), the father of modern 'skin and bones' anthropology coined the term 'Caucasian' and championed the concept of divisions of humankind based on racial varieties.

1815-1870: 'RACE' AS SPECIES

Blumenbach worked at a time when 'Negroes' – a term coined by the Spanish and Portuguese in the 16th century to describe Africans – and Native Americans were considered half-animals by Europeans. Blumenbach however did not subscribe to the view that they were inferior, arguing that in terms of physical qualities, there were, for example, as many ugly Europeans as Negroes.[7] However, the idea of the superiority of the European was to be advanced with vigour from the beginning of the 19th century, building largely upon the foundation of Blumenbach's delineation of human difference. German historian Barthold G Niebuhr is credited with being the leading figure in establishing the idea of race in this epoch. Together with Niebuhr,

Kemble in England, Taine in France, Renan the Kelt and Michelet established the popular idea that "the origins of state and nation", i.e. civilised behaviour, were rooted in the pasts of Franks and Gauls, Anglo-Saxons and Celts. The idea was that the Germanic background provided a purer race, blood and an altogether nobler people; proper human beings.

If for Blumenbach race was nothing, for Niebuhr race was everything. Early in the 19th century, Niebuhr set out to "join Enlightenment ethnography and chorography with narrative history". He wanted to show that his race remained untouched by its associations with others; for him, race was everything: race as territory, environment, poetry, revolution and class. In every area the Germanic brand of humanity was superior to others. Niebuhr became the high priest and chief advocate of northern White superiority, according to Hannaford. And one key comparison was that between the relative situations of the Caucasian and the Negro. It is worth pointing out here that missing from the analyses was any knowledge of African history: its kingdoms, kings and queens, architecture and more.[8] In post-Enlightenment Europe at least, and to those under European control, White was right, aesthetically, historically, territorially and poetically; White was right in every way that Black was not. Germanic White, the Caucasian was the superior species.

1870-1914: THE HIGHPOINT OF 'RACE' AS AN IDEA

The third period that decisively shaped race as an idea, the close of the 19th and the beginning of the 20th centuries, is regarded as the highpoint of defining this phenomenon called race. In the wake of the Darwinian evolutionary hypothesis, a plethora of writings appeared, sparking controversies about the place of the Negro in the world. Essentially, it was argued that the Negro's lowly place in the world was due to physical and intellectual incapacity and inferiority. Blumenbach's theory of the unity of the species was rejected and replaced with, for example, Dr James Hunt's evolutionary theory that "human types began with the Negro and ended (progressively) with the superior Germans".[9] In a paper given in 1863, Hunt argued that there was a greater difference in intelligence between a European and a Negro than between a gorilla and a chimpanzee. The Negro was in

Hunt's view an inferior species. It should be noted that this debate and those predating it occurred against the background of the Trans-Atlantic Slave Trade in Africans that saw between 6-10 million enslaved and shipped to the Americas for the kind of treatment usually meted out to beasts of burden. Millions met their death on the high seas or on the plantations. And it's also worth pointing out that the idea of European supremacy was to have consequences beyond the treatment of Africans; German anti-Semitism meant millions of Jews were to also perish at the altar of supremacist thinking. This supremacist ideology was also behind European expansionism.

Much more can be said than I have here, but suffice it to say that the journey of race continued on its dynamic development with great minds taking up various positions concerning the nature and significance of race. Many today will agree that whatever race is, there is no such thing as a pure race. Whether through creationist or evolutionary eyes, we have a shared history and a shared destiny.

WHAT SUSTAINS IT?

Racism is kept alive because of a number of identifiable factors. I want to identify four. First, racism as an ideology has deep roots having been fashioned over centuries and is rarely challenged at its source. Laws in Britain challenge and punish racist behaviours that are detected. However, racism at its ideological root cannot be adequately challenged by legal measures. It is never enough to challenge symptoms; the cause must be challenged and defeated or controlled. Failure to do so helps to keep racism alive. Racism says I am/we are inherently better than you. You are inferior to me/us. And I/we know you, your worth, capabilities, etc., by the colour of your skin, your nationality and your ethnic group. How ludicrous is that? But it will be the status quo as long as the ideology is unchallenged or inadequately challenged.

Second, self-interest helps to maintain racism. It is a truism, 'power is never given, it is only ever taken'. Power brings with it responsibilities and privileges, and whilst many are prepared to relinquish responsibilities, few willingly relinquish privileges. Moreover when you are part of a privileged class or group, your self-interests are wrapped up with those of others.

Third, racism is maintained by ignorance, the kind that breeds unwitting racism. The accident of birth determines what group we are born into, and it is possible to live in the world blissfully unaware of the attitudes and prejudices that are part and parcel of your context. Even when informed some find it difficult to understand, absorb and change.

Finally, racism is maintained by the complicity of its victims. Nowhere is this more true than in the context of Black and White. African American ethicist Victor Anderson, in his book 'Beyond ontological blackness',[10] argues that Whites have invented 'ontological blackness' and Blacks collude with this Blackness that Whiteness created by accepting this categorisation, even seeking to get justice and equality for the ontologically Black from the ontologically White. Anderson argues that rather than challenging the race theories based on ontological Black and White created by Enlightenment thinkers like Kant and Jefferson, African American intellectuals appropriate them to construct ontological Blackness. For Anderson, the complicity is that African Americans too easily accept the signifier Black in contradistinction to White. On a colour continuum, why should one extreme of that continuum be allowed to tell every other colour, including those closest to it, that they are Black? And why do those so called so easily reify this contrived and imposed Black ontological identity that is wholly dependent upon Whiteness for its existence?

HOW MIGHT WE RID THE CHURCH OF RACISM?

The very understanding that all humans are made in the image and likeness of God ought to be enough to ensure that in the church at least we would not treat people less favourably based on colour, nationality or any other factor. So the first step to eradicating racism from the church is for Christians to live out our 'we are one' creed. Not only are we one in our humanity, but also we are one in Christian faith. We should examine our practices, procedures and outcomes in light of non-discrimination on racial grounds. We should apply the acid test, ask victims or would be victims how they experience the church's practices and procedures. Most of all, each one of us should examine our own practices and lifestyles for signs of racism. Again apply the acid test, ask those individuals with whom we have to deal if they find us racist. Racism attacks the very core, the essence of our common humanity; it should not be practised or tolerated in the church.

A talk delivered at the Eastern Region Ministry Course, St Gabriel's Conference Centre, Ditchingham, Norfolk NR35 2DZ; Sunday 8 March 2009

1. Brian Cathcart, The Case of Stephen Lawrence, London: Penguin Books, 1999, p.405
2. I Howard Marshall, Acts: Tyndale New Testament Commentaries, Grand rapids, Michigan: Inter Varcity Press, 1980, p.370
3. Alistair McGrath, Christian Theology, Oxford: Blackwel Publishers, 1994, p.370
4. Ivan Hannaford, Race: The History of and Idea in the West, Baltimore, Maryland: Johns Hopkins University Press, 1996
5. Hannaford, p.147
6. A key figure in the development of this theory was Bartolome de Las Casas (1474-1566)
7. Hannaford, p.211
8. See Robin Walker, When we ruled, London: Every Generation Media, 2006
9. Hannaford, p.278
10. Victor Anderson, Beyond Ontological Blackness, London: Continuum, 1999

CHAPTER 5

Rethinking racism in the church

INTRODUCTION

Sadly, racism has been an integral part of the church for the longest time. It still is! This is in spite of the fact that our general reaction, particularly that of the victim, to racism is one of revulsion and intolerance. The following statement is typical,

> "Racism has no part in the Christian gospel. It contradicts our Lord's command to love our neighbour as ourselves. It offends the fundamental Christian belief that every person is made in the image of God and is equally precious in his sight. It solves no problem and creates nothing but hatred and fear."[1]

Whilst accepting the above as a truism, I suggest that since racism may always be with us in one guise or another, we may need to temper our revulsion and intolerance of racism by accepting, painfully for the victim, that we have to live with it as one of the consequences of the inherently, morally flawed human condition.[2] If racism is understood as 'a' sin, not 'the' sin above all others, we may well find that racists and the victims of racism can more readily come to God's table of reconciliation to seek for ways forward through repentance and forgiveness that lead to restorative healing. Tony Sewell runs a programme called 'Generating Genius' and he gives this tip: "Generating Genius steers clear of overt Black nationalism. We wanted the boys not to be obsessed with White racism but to have the confidence to resist it"[3]. This sums up my point quite succinctly.

Some may view this as a dangerous line to take, as giving licence to racists, especially those who practise it under the cloak of righteousness. However, as Jose Ignacio Gonzalez Faus reminds us from the Latin American situation of widespread "gratuitous, unnecessary sufferings caused by human responsibility and wrongdoing", human beings don't just sin, they are sinners.[4] And because human sinfulness, including racial sin, is 'structural', I believe that racism has to be declassified and reclassified as one sin among many. Otherwise, it holds us all prisoners, having power beyond its natural reach. Indeed, by our current thinking we run the risk of deifying racism, making it a demigod among sins, and as a consequence it rules over us – racists and victims of racism alike. I suggest therefore that there is an urgent task of normalising racism, thereby denying it pride of place among the pantheon of sins.

RACISM

According to Ivan Hannaford, the concept of 'race' as "kindred blood and colour" denoting higher and lower forms of human life did not exist in the West until the 18th century.[5] The development of this by-product of Western Enlightenment was and is a clear infringement of the biblical idea of humanity being made in God's image, having equal standing with each other (Genesis 1.27 & Acts 17.26). Racism has its roots in this construction of the ideology of race, and has been articulated variously as "belief in the superiority of a particular race; the theory that human abilities are determined by race"; "a pattern of behaviour whose consequences, intended or not, are to reinforce present racial inequalities"; and "prejudice with power".[6] Racism is clearly presumptuous on the part of the perpetrator and injurious to victims. Nonetheless it has been practised in various settings since the 18th century, even when not named as such.

RACISM IN THE CHURCH

It is possible to understand the Old Testament concept of Israel as a special people among other nations as a forerunner to modern ideas about racial superiority. Not wishing to push this thought further, there are three other examples that I wish to cite. First, slavery and the Slave Trade. The year, 2007, marks the bicentenary of the Act of Parliament to abolish the Slave Trade in the British colonies. Many have pointed out that racism was a major, if not the defining, legitimising factor of both the trade and the enslavement of Africans by Europeans since the 15th century. Richard Reddie suggests that the church was both a participant in the enslavement of and trade in Africans, benefiting institutionally and individually from their proceeds, as well as being a leading agent in the eventual successful struggle for abolition and liberation of the trade and slavery itself.[7] It is not clear how the organisation established by Jesus Christ to bring salvation based upon his own ministry (Luke 4.18) ended up participating in human oppression and degradation. One writer suggests, "White Christianity (became) the foundation of slavery and the tool of the oppressor."[8]

Second, it has now been established beyond doubt that migrating Christians, initially from the Caribbean in the Windrush era since 1948, later from Africa and Asia, were met with and have had to endure racism within the church. Some even regard this as the main reason for the establishment of Black-majority churches in Britain[9] which led Joel Edwards to protest that the Black church is not the child of rejection.[10] And recently, an internal report commissioned by the archbishops of Canterbury and York concluded that the Church of England is institutionally racist;[11] a charge made consistently by Black people in mainstream churches who have found progress and acceptability in and beyond the pew difficult.[12] Third, leaders of Black Churches have consistently complained about the treatment meted out to them by their White counterparts. In earlier times, their attempts at setting up churches in Britain saw them described as 'cults'. These three areas are a tip of the racism iceberg in the Christian church, where it is both pervasive and enduring, changing complexion and form, from overt to covert for example, but in a perverse deification, always present.

THE END OF RACISM?

I suggest that the same way in which none of us expect an end to stealing, lying, adultery and the host of wrong-doing that exist in the world, preached against in the church but ever-present none the same, there is no real reason to expect that racism will one day miraculously disappear. To expect it to do so is to be naïve, spiritually and practically. Of course, the prophetic voice of condemnation must continue to be articulated against racism, and racists must find no place in which to feel comfortable. As Robert Beckford points out, when we are rightly enraged by those who perpetrate racism upon us or others, we do not accept it, but work towards redemptive vengeance.[13] Therefore, it is important that our intolerance is one aimed at the unrighteousness of humanity, rather than the specialness of racism. As I have argued elsewhere, if we are to make progress in this complex, multi-layered society, including within the church, we must take seriously the human condition of sin. Having done so, we counter its erring ways by emphasising our divinely conceived diversity, freedom, equality and respect for self and others.[14] Racism may never come to an end, but its demigodic domination of us must.

This article first appeared in Quadrant in September 2007

1. Bishop George Cantuar, Foreword, The Passing Winter, Church Publishing House, p.v 1996.
2. At least in an Augustinian sense, human nature is believed to be inherently morally weak and predisposed to sinfulness of all sorts. See, Alister McGrath, Christian Theology, Blackwell Publishers, 1994, p.371.
3. Tony Sewell, *Generating Genius: Black Boys in Love, Ritual and Schooling*, Trentham Books, 2009.
4. Jose Ignacio Gonzalez Faus, 'Sin' in Jon Sobrino & Ignacio Ellacuria (eds), Systematic Theology, SCM Press, 1996, p194-204.
5. Ivan Hannaford, Race – the history of an idea in the West, John Hopkins University Press, 1996, p.235.
6. Racism in British Society, Catholic Association for Racial Justice, 1993, pp. 4&5.
7. Richard Reddie, Abolition, Lion Hudson, 2007.
8. John L Wilkinson, Church in Black and White, Saint Andrew Press, 1993, p.63
9. Mark Sturge, Look what the Lord has done, Scripture Union, 2005.
10. Joel Edwards (ed) in Let's Praise Him again, Kingsway Publications, 1992
11. http://www.telegraph.co.uk/news/main.jhtml?xml=/news/2007/06/17/nchurch117.xml
12. See several articles in Anthony Reddie (ed), Black Theology – an international journal, Equinox; e.g. volume 4 number 2, 2006
13. Robert Beckford, God of the Rahtid, Darton Longman & Todd, 2001
14. Joe Aldred, Respect – understanding Caribbean British Christianity, Epworth, 2005

CHAPTER 6

The human face of God

I am now totally convinced that every Christian needs to embrace a mental and physical image of Jesus, the incarnate Son of God, as someone who looks like them. This is particularly true for Black people generally, and Black Britons in particular, who have undergone centuries of conditioning by seeing Jesus portrayed relentlessly as a White European, with the devil and his imps as Black. Let me begin this talk with three personal stories.

First, during the early part of my life, the colour of Jesus was not a major issue for me. But it became so after I read the Black American theologian James Cone's bold claim that "Jesus is Black". Cone's argument ran along the line that since God is to be found among the poor and oppressed, his incarnation in Jesus of necessity has to be expressed as one of those poor and oppressed people. And given that Black people are the poor and oppressed in America, Jesus must be Black. It is an interesting, if parochial, Christological view, but it certainly got me thinking. Since that time during the 1970s, I have discovered biblical scholars like Cain Hope Felder who argue that the Middle East of Jesus' day was an extension of Africa, and that the people of that area were phenotypically Afroasian, or people of colour. This kind of talk turned my little world upside down, since up to that time my mental image of Jesus was as a White European male. After all this is how he appeared in my Bible, in the books I had read and in the paintings I had seen.

Second, quite recently, I came across a website with the face of Jesus depicted in the shape and complexion of several ethnic, national, historic and ideological identities. These computer generated images include Jesus as the light of the world, the Bar Code Jesus, Jesus in the Shroud of Turin, Jesus the Revolutionary, Jesus the Liberator, Jesus the Eastern Icon and the Forensic Image of Jesus which was developed for the 'Son of Man' television series. This was the series which culminated in a depiction of what a 1st century Galilean might have looked like. With millions of others, I recall being glued to my television screen to see what a computer would say Jesus might have looked like. This approach produced a rather unglamorous, rugged man of colour. The 'Jesus was Black' brigade felt vindicated and happy. Further web searches turned up additional images of Jesus as a person of colour, again in various forms.

Third, a few years ago, I came across and acquired a version of the Bible called the 'Original African Heritage Bible'. This was in fact the traditional King James Version of the Bible, but with an African overlay. By this I mean that it had an introduction and preface that sought to highlight what the editors call giving credit to ancient Africa and her peoples for their unquestionable and authenticated contributions made towards the formation and development of Judaism, Christianity and the Holy Bible. The authors of the Original African Heritage Bible have gone through and highlighted the passages, references, people and places in the Bible depicting African-Asiatic people. In fact, I discovered that once you begin to look at the Bible like this, the question is not 'where are the Blacks in the Bible?' but 'where are the Whites?' A feature of this Bible is that its iconography depicts Black people. In fact, everybody in this Bible is Black. Fantastic! For the first time I had a Bible with images of people that looked like me. I was quite enchanted by a picture of Jesus that looked more like the great West Indian batsman Viv Richards than the blonde haired, blue-eyed European I had grown up seeing – the Charlton Heston figure, much maligned by the Black Civil Rights activist Malcolm X. Viv Richards starring as Jesus in a movie, now there is an idea.

Anyway, I carried this Bible around with me everywhere I went and showed it off. I preached, taught, exhorted and studied from it. I encouraged others to buy their own copies. Then I realised that not everybody was as excited about Black imagery of biblical characters as I was. To my great surprise, many Black Christians were most upset by the idea of a Black Jesus, even hostile! Some said to me, "Oh it does not matter what colour Jesus was". I said, "Well if it doesn't matter, why are you upset if it is Black?"

To me all of these developments were very refreshing, because they support the notion that all people of the earth are at liberty to embrace an imagery of Jesus that looks like them. It may be that this appeals to me particularly because I have a long-standing angst against the monolithic and misleading Europeanisation of the Christ image and the damage I believe this has caused, and continues to cause for Black, or non-White, people.

Then I realised that although I had grown up with it, I had not taken sufficient stock of just how engrained the White imagery of Jesus and other Bible characters was, particularly in the Black Christian psyche. It seems that deep in the subconscious, Black Christians were worshipping a Jesus whose features are akin to their White European slave masters, colonial rulers and modern day oppressors. So in spite of the sordid history, Blacks still believe that White is superior and so God, the most superior of all, has to be White too. Somehow it seems that the dominant presence of Whites had easily transmitted itself into the God-figure for Black Christians and the White icons epitomised this.

I began to notice in Black Churches, if there were any icons at all they were White. Only once did I visit a church in Handsworth, Birmingham, which displayed a picture of the Black Madonna and Child. This also happened to be the church of the emerging radical Black British theologian, Dr Robert Beckford, now famous for his depiction of Jesus with Rastafarian dreadlocks. This apart, it is clear that Caribbean-British Christian worshippers are more at ease with White imagery of God than Black in their places of worship.

I notice too that in the homes of my church brethren and friends there is nearly always a picture of a White Jesus. There is the Sacred Heart picture of Jesus, the Good Shepherd Jesus and Jesus at the Last Supper with his twelve White disciples. With words like, 'Jesus is the unseen guest at every meal' and 'I am the Good Shepherd', these images allude to a sense of security, authority, care and salvation. In Black Christians' homes, these pictures tend to be strategically situated in hallways or living rooms in ways that have Jesus 'looking down' on everyone, as if to say, "don't worry, I'm here, I'm in charge".

To cap it all, on recent trips to Jamaica, to funerals of my mother, father and recently my brother, I noticed how White images of Jesus and angelic beings are utilised to bring peace and assurance to relatives of the deceased. In the case of my brother's funeral, there was a picture of Jesus and his disciples in his casket! My mournful disposition during the funeral did not permit me to challenge this. Yes, in Jamaica where the White proportion of the population is a mere 1%, the 99% Black, Asian and mixed heritage people still seem to need White imagery of heavenly beings to keep them feeling assured that all is well over on the other side where their loved ones have gone. I protested to the owner of the funeral parlour, but he didn't seem to get the point.

It seems to me that the Renaissance painters and their ideological associates of the Enlightenment have done a masterful job of brainwashing the world with the notion that the biblical story originated and was lived out in Europe and that all the key players on that stage were White. We have all imbibed the idea that only the devil and the fallen angels were Black. Of course, Britain and much of Western Europe had many years of imperialism and colonial rule through which to impose this ideology upon its mainly Black subjects.

Most of us know now that the biblical drama was played out on the African-Asiatic stage and that Europe, as we know it today, had only a peripheral role. As Cain Hope Felder puts it, the Sweet Little Jesus Boy of the Negro Spiritual was in fact quite Black. How else, for example, could Jesus' parents have been convinced by the angel to seek refuge from Pharaoh in Egypt? Imagine a White European family attempting to hide in Black Africa!

People do say to me and others who point out these historical matters, "what does it mater what colour Jesus was?" Maybe you are asking the same question. Well, let me tell you why it matters. Imagine that you lived in a world where people of darker hue were widely disadvantaged in matters of world trade, indebtedness, food shortages, water shortages, ill-health, unemployment, poor housing, underachievement in education, and the list goes on. Imagine that when you run for refuge in the church, you found that the White Christians in the church exhibited the same colour prejudices and racist exclusion as were prevalent in the wider world. Imagine a world in which almost everything seems to be against you and you turn to God, only to discover that all the images of God you can find are the same as the White people who oppress and exclude you. I imagine you would conclude that there is no hope for you in a world like that.

For hundreds of years of slavery, indentured labour and colonial rule, people of colour have been told and made to feel that Black is evil and White is good. This is confirmed by portraying the devil as

Black and God as White. I believe that the time is ripe for portraying the incarnate Jesus in the image of the people portraying him. Seeing the image of God in the image of yourself is particularly important in a world in which the group that sets itself up as superior to all others has also imposed upon the world the image of God in their image. To use your power in the world to deify your race is understandable but wrong. And every Black person should remove, forthwith, every White image of Christ in their homes and churches and replace them with images similar to those in the Original African Heritage Bible. Not to replace White imagery of Jesus and other heavenly beings with Black ones is, I believe, to continue to live out a self-imposed Black inferiority that in a neo-colonial way subjugates itself to White supremacy.

Excuses about 'colour doesn't matter' are mere avoidance mechanisms that keep the Black/White inferior/superior dichotomy alive. Colonial hangover is still a reality in the church as in the rest of society for too many today. The Bible says it is for freedom that Christ has set us free. This means for me that even though we may have been in bondage to a superior power, salvation in Christ sets us free so that we are in bondage to no one; we are inferior to no one, and we have the responsibility to set others free too.

The great Bob Marley sang, "emancipate yourself from mental slavery, none but ourselves can free our minds". It is not up to White people, Christians or not, to free Black people from feelings of inferiority; it is up to Black people to free ourselves, and this freedom starts in our minds. By renewing our minds in Christ we come to know that in him all are one. The only superior one is God. And the Christ who came amongst us in the Incarnation, had to come in the image of all of us, or he is in the image of none of us.

First broadcast in a BBC Radio 4 Lent Talk Series

CHAPTER 7

Responding to the legacy of the slave trade

How ought we to respond to the legacy of the Transatlantic Slave Trade? During this year (2007), I've been involved in several discussions dealing with this question of responding to the contemporary legacies of the Slave Trade. This includes my own writings in newspapers and periodicals, participating in discussions on radio and importantly discussions among African Caribbean communities. The latter includes a discussion in Birmingham on BBC Radio West Midlands. It was a most poignant, difficult and at times angry discussion. The anger of many in the African Caribbean community is rooted in the unease with how easily the poacher can turn gamekeeper. So that from John Hawkins the villain, to William Wilberforce the saint, one thing is consistent: Black invisibility; even twelve million Blacks. In this very problematic bicentenary commemoration year, White people in particular need to make every effort to avoid the scenario of 'heads I win, tails you lose'.

The 'Set all Free' abolition project of Churches Together in England (CTE) offers us two broad headings under which we might consider our response. First, 'by working to effect healing and reconciliation'. How might we do this? Let me suggest that we might do well to focus on that old Christian word, 'atonement'. This means 'to cover', 'to appease', 'to placate' or 'to cancel'. Atonement is brought about by sacrifice as exemplified by Jesus' death for human sin, but it brings about peace and closure. So what might be a suitable act or series of acts of atonement responses to this history of psychological, spiritual, economic, social and political degradation we call the Slave Trade?

First of all, let's use an appropriate phrase to describe what we are talking about. The Atlantic Ocean did not enslave anybody, so I suggest renaming this shameful trade the 'European Slave Trade in Africans'. Then, our Prime Minister might move from equivocally expressing "deep sorrow" for Britain's involvement in the Trade, to unequivocally saying "sorry". Western Europe's leaders might recognise the devastation caused by the Slave Trade, slavery and colonialism by seriously and respectfully engaging with African and Caribbean leaders about a way forward in true partnership. How about erecting a monument in central London as a reminder to present and future generations never again to enslave our fellow humans and thereby deface the image of God in man. When abolition was agreed, the planters were compensated to the tune of £20 million. The enslaved Africans got nothing. So, how about establishing this bicentenary year an 'atonement fund' of £20 million to begin with, for the benefit of the descendents of the survivors of the trade, to offer bursaries to study at higher degree levels, and as business seed funding. Then how about a public holiday for everybody; we could colonise an existing Bank Holiday and call it 'Freedom Day', symbolising our vision of a world in which all are free. Then let's all take up Set all Free's challenge to take action to end all modern forms of slavery. And let the church take the lead in rooting out racism from our midst as an example to the wider society.

I feel the need to warn us that if we are what the book of James warns against, 'hearers and not doers', if we mouth remorse but do not repent and make restitution, if we talk the talk but do not walk the walk, there will continue to be for years to come an angry, disenfranchised part of our community whose presence will be a constant reminder of our failure to truly respond to the enduring legacies of the European Slave Trade in Africans.

Talk given at Durham cathedral Saturday 24 March 2007

Part 2

BIBLE

CHAPTER 8

Recognising the 400th anniversary of the KJV

INTRODUCTION

I want to express my appreciation for the opportunity to make this presentation in your National Convention. It's a privilege I do not take lightly. I also want to say how much I appreciate presiding bishop Eric Brown and his staff, in particular Leony Titus and Phyllis Thompson, for the excellent support I receive in the ecumenical work I do at Churches Together in England. I hope you are aware that the New Testament Church of God is a significant force for good in this nation, and I applaud your Church's unselfish contribution to the wider church's mission and response to the prayer of Jesus in St John 17 for the unity of his church on earth.

Turning to my assignment for this afternoon, let me begin by saying that in Bible terms, I think in the King James Version (KJV). I grew up reading it and to this day when I use a Bible concordance or dictionary, my vocabulary comes from the KJV. It's kind of my biblical mother tongue. I suspect this is true for some of you at least. It is appropriate then that we join millions in this country and around the world, from all walks of life, in marking the 400th anniversary of the KJV. Prince Charles speaks for many in his Foreword to the 400th Anniversary Edition of the KJV when he says, "what it stood for when first published, and what it continues to embody, is something very close to my heart: a lyrical beauty that conveys a deep sense of the sacred".

Today, I want to take us on a short journey looking at what preceded the KJV and how it came about. I will end by situating the KJV in today's world of multiple translations of the Bible. Expect a few surprises along the way. I begin by asking the obvious question, what exactly is the King James Version? Put simply, it's an English translation of the Bible that first appeared in 1611. In the translators' note to the reader in the original edition, titled 'The Translators to the Reader', they said, "We never thought from the beginning that we would need to make a new translation, or even to make a bad one into a good one, but to make a good one better, or out of many good ones to make one principal good one, not justly to be objected to. This has been our endeavour, our goal". The end product of the translators' work, according to one commentator, is simply the most celebrated and important book in the English-speaking world. One indication of the esteem in which the KJV has been historically held is that in her coronation year of 1953, Queen Elizabeth commanded that a copy of the KJV be given to every child in Britain. Could this happen today? I wonder.

ABOUT THE BIBLE GENERALLY

The KJV of 1611 was and is part of a historical context of God's self-declaration of the divine in human language. It was not the first or last translation of the Bible, in fact, as the chart below shows, the KJV was a bit of a 'Johnny-come-lately'.

The biblical history is set within a wider history of the emergence of sacred texts, some of which predate the Biblical records. I refer here, for example, to the Sumerian's Locust Charm the Epic of Gilgamesh texts (circa 2000 BC), and ancient Egyptian Pyramid texts (circa 2400 BC). You'll find references to these and others in the British Library. Of course all world faiths have their sacred texts. The Christian Bible was written over a period of approximately 2000 years by over some forty authors from backgrounds as varied as fishermen, shepherds, kings, and intellectuals such as Paul. The Christian Bible is rooted in the Hebrew Scriptures, including the understanding of divine inspiration which is the belief that "all Scripture is given by inspiration of God, and is profitable for doctrine, for reproof, for correction, for instruction in righteousness" (2 Timothy 3.16). And it's this inspired text that the KJV and others bring to us in our language. The process has been long, arduous and costly, not least in human lives.

Historically, there has been a swirling pool of writings, translations, revisions, disputations and affirmations which reminds us of how in creation God turned chaos into order. The results are the canons of Old Testament, New Testament and the books known in Jamaica as

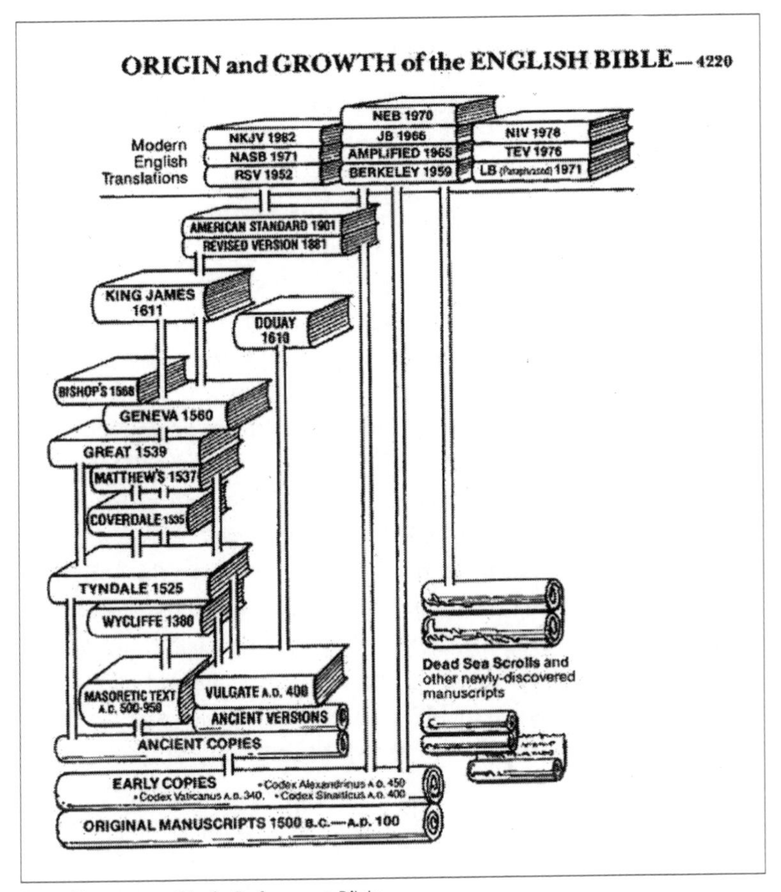

From Thompson Chain Reference Bible

the Macabbees, better known as the Deutero-canonical or apocryphal writings; these are surrounded by many other works by church Fathers like Origen, Augustine and others. And because much of the world of the early centuries was under Roman rule, many translations were in Latin. Up to the 5th century AD these included the Codex Vaticanus, Codex Sinaiticus and the Codex Alexandrinus. The authoritative Masoretic Hebrew texts of the Jewish Bible appeared between the 6th -10th centuries AD and have been widely used as the basis for translations of the Old Testament in Protestant and Catholic Bibles. Biblically, differences have developed between Orthodox Churches, Catholic Churches and Protestant Churches in the West. By 500 AD the Bible had been translated into over 500 different languages.

SOME NOTABLE PRE-KJV TRANSLATIONS

Probably the first Bible of note for us was that of 382 AD when Pope Damasus 1, bishop of Rome, commissioned St Jerome to make a revision of the old Latin versions; this resulted in a definitive Latin version known as the Vulgate Bible, the versio vulgata, or 'the commonly used translation'. It remained popular for over 1000 years until the 16th century. The Catholic Church did not encourage lay people to read the Bible, and in league with the state from circa 600 AD made it illegal in the Roman Empire, punishable by death, to publish the Bible in any other language but Latin.

One person among many who challenged these restrictions was John Wycliffe, Oxford scholar, theologian and lay preacher. He wanted the common person to have access to the Bible and in their own language. In 1382, the Wycliffe Bible was produced by Wycliffe and his colleagues. It was a hand-written version of Old and New Testaments based upon the Vulgate and the Masoretic texts. The Church authorities hated this and although Wycliffe died naturally he was posthumously convicted of heresy and at the command of Pope Martin V, his body was exhumed in 1428, his remains burned and the ashes cast into the River Swift that flows through his home town of Lutterworth. Wycliffe was charged with having "made the Bible common and open to the laity and to women" (Gordon Campbell p9).

The invention in 1455 AD of the printing press by Johannes Gutenberg meant that books including the Bible could be reproduced faster than hand-written versions like Wycliffe's. The Bible in Latin was the first to be printed.

In 1526 AD the Tyndale New Testament Bible was published in English. It was the work of another remarkable man, William Tyndale of Oxford and Cambridge who is regarded as the father of the English Bible. Tyndale was fluent in Greek, Latin, Hebrew, German, Spanish and French, and was also determined to publish the Bible in the people's languages, especially in English. He defied the Pope, telling him that he was determined that if God spared his life he would cause a "boy that driveth the plough to know more of the Scripture that thou dost" (Gordon p10). His Bible was particularly incendiary because its pocket size made it easy to transport and smuggle. Tyndale fled for his life to Germany, but the King of England had thousands of copies of his

Bible confiscated and burned. Finally, in 1536, Tyndale was himself burned at the stake as a heretic.

In 1535 AD, the Coverdale Bible was published. Myles Coverdale's Bible was the first complete Bible printed in English; it had 80 Books in all, Old Testament, New Testament and the Apocrypha. While the Catholic Church still banned non-Latin Bibles, the new Church of England and the English monarchy were more tolerant. The Coverdale Bible depicted King Henry VIII on the cover, sitting enthroned and handing out Bibles to his Church of England bishops, with the laity kneeling in attendance. How things had changed! But had they? We have to factor into the equation that there were lots of political games between the powers of church and state; both were divided and in open warfare with each other and within each other, and which side of the 'war' was safe depended entirely on what was going on and who was winning at the time. Also, people were running to and fro for refuge in Europe and elsewhere.

The Coverdale Bible was quickly followed by the Matthew Bible of 1537 published by John Rogers. He was caught however in the cross-fire between the Catholic Church, the Protestants and Dissenters, and the Monarchy and was burnt alive for his non-Catholic, Protestant faith. However, the Church of England with King Henry VIII as its head, authorised the Matthew Bible dedicated to the king and bearing his image, and with Thomas Cromwell's help the Matthew Bible was ordered to be read in all 8,000 parish churches. The Matthew Bible was followed by the Great Bible in 1539, so called because of its size, 15" x 9", deliberately intended to replace the Matthew Bible in churches. Somehow at long last, the Bible that had been locked away in Latin from the English speaking populous now found its way into every parish church of the Church of England.

Just as people in England thought it was safe to print and read the Bible in English, King Edward VI (1547-1553) was succeeded on the English throne by Queen Mary I in 1553. A confirmed Catholic, she brought an end to the printing of the Bible in English and their use in churches. She killed John Rogers, the publisher of the Matthew Bible, as part of a widespread persecution of Protestants. She is reputed to have had over 280 religious dissenters burned at the stake. Non-Catholics fled again for their lives, mostly to Europe. Queen Mary I's reign was short-lived and she was replaced by Queen Elizabeth I in

1558. This heralded the return of many from exile some of whom attracted the nickname the 'Puritans' because of their staunch anti-papal beliefs. While in exile in Geneva, some including William Whittingham, Miles Coverdale and John Knox, published the very influential 'anti-Catholic' Geneva Bible in 1560, also known as the Puritan's Bible. For the first time in an English language Bible numbered verses to each chapter was added. It was dedicated to Queen Elizabeth and contained the 80 Old and New Testaments books and the Apocrypha. This was the Bible the Pilgrims took to America on the Mayflower in 1620. The Geneva Bible's margin notes offended the papacy, episcopacy and the Monarchy, and King James thought it subversive of royal authority (Campbell p 28). However, the Geneva Bible was extremely popular with the masses, undergoing 70 editions and remained in print from 1560 until 1640.

We come to the last two translations before the KJV. First the Bishop's Bible published in 1568; so called because of the large number of bishops on the revision committee. Based on the Great Bible, this was a direct response to the Geneva Bible of the Puritans. This was the bishops of the Church of England flexing their muscles and it became the Bible authorised to be read in cathedrals and churches in England. The final translation I want to mention in this survey is the Douay-Reims Bible that was published by the Catholic Church. Although Catholics were still not encouraged to read the Bible privately, the Church needed an English translation antidote for its people against the popular Geneva Bible. The Douay-Reims' New Testament was completed in 1582 and the Old Testament in 1610. It was technically good but not a popular read. An example of why is evident in the rendering of 'daily bread' in the Lord's Prayer, as "super-substantial bread", and Jesus is said to have "exinanited Himself" for 'emptied himself' in Philippians 2.8.

As you may note from some of what's been said, gradually, the Bible began to be seen by the powers that be as a political tool, not to be banned but to be used to unite their disparate peoples and interests, and strengthen their power base. Rather than prevent people from reading it, the monarchy could simply vouchsafe the messages contained in the Bible proper and in the margins and ensure they served the ruler's best interests. Gradually, Bibles had been permitted, legalised in England and set forth with the monarch's most gracious licence. In it the King or Queen of England could be depicted as supreme head of the Church, defender of the faith. By 1611, the practice of appointing Bibles to be read in churches was well established. The Bible had come a long way.

THE EMERGENCE OF THE KJV

At the beginning of the 17th century the Geneva or the Puritan's Bible was in popular use for private study, and the Bishop's Bible was read in the churches of England. But as we've seen, the Catholics, the bishops of the Church of England and the monarchy did not like the popular Geneva Bible because of its considered anti-papal, anti-Episcopal, and anti-monarchist inclusions. In the background, the Puritans bewailed the manner in which the Church of England was still too Catholic and they craved a more Protestant Church, void of papal influences and free from state control. In time, King James of Scotland also became King of England. As the new king made his way to claim the English throne, some dissenting Puritans took the opportunity to make representation to him.

In what was termed, 'The Millenary Petition' with over 1000 signatories, the king was presented with the Puritans' demand. In it they respectfully outlined their desire for the redress of divers abuses of the Church. The Puritans' petition stressed throughout that they were not separatists or schismatics, but expressed their feelings that the English Reformation had not gone far enough to purge the Church of England from the errors of the Roman Catholic Church. Their demands fell into four main categories: Church services, Church ministers, Church livings and maintenance and Church discipline. Each was followed by a long list of requests. Some of their specific demands included that women should not be allowed to baptise converts; removal of popish rites, ceremonies and vestments; clergy to be allowed to marry; clergy to be educated; that doctrines be grounded in Scripture not the authority of clergy and church tradition. They asked that all other abuses yet remaining and practiced in the Church of England that were not agreeable to the Scriptures be changed, amended or qualified.

The new king, keen to appease his new subjects and having a love for theological debate, quickly agreed to convene a conference to discuss the Puritans' petition. This became an early opportunity for the king to consolidate his position as head of the Church of England. And so a three-day conference, initially planned for October 1603 but postponed due to an outbreak of the plague, took place 15th-17th January 1604 at Hampton Court Palace with the King calling together the leaders of the Church of England, a selection of archbishops, archdeacons, bishops, deans and some moderate Puritans. The incapacitated Archbishop of Canterbury, John Whitgift with the Bishop of London Richard Bancroft, who succeeded him as Archbishop of Canterbury later that year, headed up the Bishops' delegation, while John Rainolds, President of Corpus Christi College Oxford, led the Puritans. As you might expect, Archbishops Whitgift and Bancroft strongly opposed the Puritans in the conference, with King James seeking compromise. For example, the Puritans got their way that women should not conduct baptisms but the Bishops got theirs that Puritan ministers would be compelled to abide by the 39 Articles of the Anglican Church. King James pronounced himself "well satisfied" with the outcome of the conference.

The crowning glory of the Hampton Court conference for the Puritans was that on day two their leader John Rainolds successfully proposed an item that was not even on the agenda, "that there might be a new translation of the Bible, because those that were allowed previously were corrupt, and not answerable to the truth of the original". This was an interesting proposal because the popular Bible at the time was the Puritan's own Geneva Bible, but of course it was not commissioned for use in churches, only the Bishop's Bible was. This was conceivably a ploy to replace the Bishop's Bible with another of Puritan leaning as the Bible to be read in churches. The Bishops saw through the plan and disapproved of the idea of a new Bible, content that the one authorised for use in the churches was theirs. The king with an eye on a win-win compromise welcomed the idea of a new translation – and it was agreed. A new translation of the Bible emerging from a conference called for by the Puritans and chaired by the king provided a big concession to the Puritans and suited the king very well indeed. The Bishops were overruled and put in their place by the king, their boss, and a new translation was authorised that would be dedicated to the king, head of the Church of England.

The king though, calling upon all his wisdom and guile and knowing that the Puritans had got their way appeased the Bishops by agreeing that Bishop Bancroft, acting Archbishop of Canterbury, would oversee the process of selection of translators and the translation. The process was to be rigorous and the very brightest people available in England were to be chosen to undertake this task, drawing upon all the best available translations and original texts that could be found, including The Bishop's Bible, Tyndale's, Matthew's, Coverdale's and the Great Bible. Fifteen rules were decided upon to guide the new translation; some of them deliberately designed to ensure the Puritans did not get their way and the worst excesses of their Geneva Bible not to be carried over into the new translation. Time and space do not permit me to share all fifteen rules, but in summary, the new translation was to follow the Bishop's Bible as much as possible with as little altered as possible, with the aim not to make a new translation but to make a good one (the Bishop's Bible) better. In anti-Puritan style, the rules stipulated for example, that the word 'church' was not to be translated 'congregation', 'wash' was to be rendered 'baptise', 'elder' or 'senior' to be rendered 'bishop', and 'minister', to be rendered 'priest'.

Chapters were not to be altered; there were to be no marginal notes except to Hebrew or Greek terms that cannot be suitably translated into English; there were to be translators' groups or companies that would take responsibilities for particular parts of the Bible headed by the king's professors of Hebrew or Greek at Westminster, Chester, Oxford and Cambridge universities. These were Lancelot Andrewes dean of Westminster, Willian Barlow dean of Chester, Regius Professors of Hebrew – Edward Lively at Cambridge and John Harding at Oxford, and Regius Professors of Greek – Andrew Downes at Cambridge and John Perrine at Oxford. There were six companies of approximately 10-12 experts, two each from Westminster, Oxford and Cambridge. They were a truly exceptional gathering of the educated elite, believers who it is said prayed always before beginning their work. At a time when education was truly a privilege for the privileged, those who had it, had a lot of it. For example, one of the translators, Richard Brett, was fluent in Latin, Greek, Hebrew, Aramaic, Arabic and Ethiopic. They were bright, charitable and prayerful but not perfect; more than one of them was renowned for their liking of the bottle, sharp temper and vindictiveness.

The rules governing this translation were unprecedented in their rigour. The companies of translators worked collaboratively. The result was that after seven years a new translation emerged, magnificent in its accuracy, that included the Old and New Testament and the Deutero-canonical or Apocrypha. As an aside, these extra-canonical books were gradually dropped from the Protestant Bible during and after the Reformation, and by the 20th century had pretty much disappeared from most Protestant Bibles on sale to the general public. Historically, these extra-biblical writings were included in the Bible whilst noting that there were controversies about their inspired status. The main approach was to view them as useful for study but not inspired. In the Geneva Bible they were accompanied by the statement, "useful for knowledge of history and instruction of godly manners". I think this is the correct approach to them even today.

We get a sense of some of the challenges the translators faced by looking at an example in Gordon Campbell's book 'Bible: the story of the King James Bible'. On a question of textual authority, 2 Timothy 3.16 is a good example. In Wycliffe's version it is rendered: "All scripture is given by inspiration of God, and is profitable to doctrine, to reprove, to correction, to instruction which is righteousness". However in Tyndale's it says, "For all scripture gave by inspiration of God is profitable to teach to improve to amend and to instruct in righteousness". Campbell points out that there is a potentially serious difference here in that Wycliffe's version asserts that all Scripture is inspired, whereas Tyndale's is open to the interpretation that only some Scripture is inspired. The KJV largely sides with Wycliffe's version. Challenges like this was a constant companion of the translators. They had to wrestle with questions about verbal and literal translation of God's Word from the original texts in Hebrew, Aramaic and Greek, but of course by 1604 there were little or no original texts to work from. They had the Hebrew and Greek texts available in the Septuagint of the 2nd century BC and Massoretic text of the 6th-10th centuries AD, plus others that were authoritative but not original. The translators of the KJV took the pragmatic view that by comparing and contrasting what was available, dating back as far as possible, they came as close as possible to the original words of God as written or spoken by the original authors, and that, as explained in the Translators to the Reader, a translation of the Bible "containeth, nay is the Word of God: as the King's speech uttered in Parliament, being translated into French, Dutch, Italian and Latin, is still the King's speech". It's worth remembering too that the KJV was translated with reading out loud in mind, hence the determination to make it as rhythmic and monosyllabic as possible. Check, for example, "Our Father, which art in heaven, hallowed be thy name, thy kingdom come…"

Although not apparent to the reader, the KJV we have today is not the 1611 version which underwent extensive modern revisions - in 1629, 1638, 1653, 1701, 1762 and 1769. It is on the 1769 version by Dr Benjamin Blayney of Oxford that today's KJV is based. It is reckoned that there were some 75,000 changes between the 1611 edition and the one in 1769. These were in the main attention to spellings, references, names, punctuations, printing errors and updating the English language as it evolved. As L M Haines says, "trying to hold on to an English style of the past is not a virtue if it puts a veil over God's Words". As with so much else in life, the only constant has been change; not change in the unchanging Word of God, but in its translations into changing human tongues.

WHERE TO NOW FOR THE KJV?

The KJV of 1611 was written in the Elizabethan English of that time, which most of us would struggle to read today. It is often assumed that the language of 'ye', 'thee' and 'thou' represent the spoken English of 1611. However, scholars tell us that by the time of the publication of the KJV, this kind of language was already archaic and spoken only in the conservative educated parts of society the translators lived in. This may help explain why the KJV was not an instant hit with readers. It took some fifty years until circa 1660, after the civil war and the restoration of the English monarchy, before the KJV could have been considered to have replaced both the Bishop's Bible for reading in churches and the Geneva Bible as the popular Bible for personal reading. Much more could be said, for example, about the politics of printing the Bible, which for a long time required Royal permission, and how some printers were bankrupted by bad business or sabotage, a few ending up in prison. And of course the revisions of the KJV continued to purge blemishes and keep pace with scholarship.

But it's worth saying something about printing errors. Printing in the early days was onerous, not the sophisticated art it is today, and as a result mistakes were easy to make. In one version, the 'not' was omitted from the seventh commandment so making adultery compulsory! There was the printing error that led to the Judas Bible because Matthew 26.36 read, "Then cometh Judas went with them unto a place called Gethsemane", instead of then cometh Jesus. Psalm 119.161 read in a 1612 KJV version, "printers have persecuted me" instead of princes. In 1 Corinthians 6.9, a 'not' was missing so it read, "know ye not that the unrighteous shall inherit the kingdom of God?" In 1795 another version swapped filled with killed and Mark 7.27 read, "Let the children first be killed". In 1810, a version swapped wife with life and rendered Luke 14.26, "If any man hate not his own wife also".

But when all the politicking and chicanery was done, and the arguments by vested interests and conscientious objectors against the KJV were brought into perspective, one 17th century commentator said this, "after long expectation, and great desire, came forth the new translation of the Bible (most beautifully printed) by a select and competent number of divines appointed for that purpose; not being many, lest one should trouble another, and yet many, lest, in any, things might haply escape them…so that their industry, skilfulness, piety, and discretion hath herin bound the Church unto them in a debt of special remembrance and thankfulness. These, with Jacob, rolled away the stone from the mouth of the well of life, so that now even Rachels, weak women, may freely come, both to drink themselves and to water the flocks of their families at the same" (Campbell p.126).

There are of course those who ascribe infallibility to the KJV; I believe this to be misguided. The KJV is an inestimably good translation but it is no more or less the Word of God than what went before it or what has come after it. It has given society some of the most memorable phrases because of the manner in which the translators chose their words, in simplicity and profundity. "At my wits end" comes from Psalm 107.27; "the skin of my teeth" from Psalm 19.20; "salt of the earth" from Matthew 5.13; "thorn in the flesh" from 1 Corinthians 12.7; "writing on the wall" from Daniel 5.5; "leopard cannot change its spots" from Jeremiah 13.23; "fly in the ointment" from Ecclesiastes 10.1; "go the second mile" from Matthew 5.41; "you can't take it with you" from Ecclesiastes 5.15. For centuries this book has been a centrepiece for legislators, writers, religious and cultural shapers. And as Britain spread its imperialist wings across the world, especially in

Africa, Asia and the Caribbean, it took the KJV with it, which explains why so many of us from former colonies encountered the KJV. We fell in love with it. It's been used to oppress and to liberate, and as one commentator says, other translations may engage the mind but the KJV is the Bible of the heart. Today it is still the most sold version of the Bible, with millions printed and sold every year.

For me, the KJV stands as a beacon among translations and we rightly celebrate its 400th anniversary in 2011. It sits on my shelf, several copies of it, alongside many contemporary translations, among them: Revised Version (1881), American Standard Version (1901), Revised Standard Version (1952), Berkley (1959), Amplified Bible (1965), Jerusalem Bible (1966), New English Bible (1970), New American Standard Bible (1971), Living Bible (1971), Today's English Version (1976), Good News Bible (1976), New International Version (1978), New King James Version (1982), New Revised Standard Version (1989), Contemporary English Version (1995), The Message (2002) and more. Together they represent the one Word of God written in different dialects. There is no need, indeed I would argue it is unwise, to restrict oneself to a version, especially one rooted in the English of the 17th century. Tyndale's ambition that everyone, from the ploughboy to the pope, should have access to the Bible in their common language has truly come to pass. It is now for us to read, be enriched by and obey the words of Scripture that call us to be not readers of the Word only, but doers also. Happy anniversary KJV! Amen.

A presentation delivered at the New Testament Church of God National Convention, Bethel Convention Centre, Sunday 31 July 2011

Sources
Various Internet sources
David Spriggs, 'The King James Bible' Lecture
Leyland M Haines, Translation and the Greek Text
Terence Copley, The Bible: The Story of the Book
Gordon Campbell, Bible: The Story of the King James Version
The Holy Bible, King James Authorised Version, 400th Anniversary Edition
Lord Melvyn Bragg, *The Book of Books: The Radical Impact of the King James Bible 1611-2011*

Part 3

BLACK CHURCH

CHAPTER 9

Black churches: contributing to cohesion or polarisation?

INTRODUCTION

I estimate that there may be as many as 500,000 committed Black Christians in the UK, and for better or for worse, I am one example of what the Black Church they have created in Britain produces. Since the autumn of 1968, this socio-religious space has provided me with somewhere of "shelter and rescue", as Robert Beckford calls it. And because, as Beckford also says, "at the heart of the Black Church is a desire to transform and empower",[1] as well as being sheltered and rescued, I have also been coached and corrected, moulded and made, prayed for and anointed, until today I am what I am: abundantly clear about my identity as a Christian man of Caribbean British heritage. Please forgive me if in this presentation I am less than sublimely objective, dispassionate and coolly intellectual. Like Richard Reddie in his recent book, "I cannot pretend to be a disinterested observer".[2]

I want to take time to investigate this topic from my own perspective before inviting your observations, input, and even your contradictions. First, I will examine the notion of 'Black Churches', then I will turn my attention to the second question posed by my topic, namely, whether these churches contribute to cohesion or polarisation.

BLACK CHURCHES

Let me begin then by addressing what I mean by 'Black Churches'. Neither of the two terms 'Black' or 'Church' is easy to define, so let me set my own parameters. By Black, I mean people of African and Caribbean heritages, plus others who voluntarily describe themselves as Black, such as some Asians. The debate about the meaning of Black has been conducted with vigour in recent years, often viewed through sociological, political and theological prisms. Sociologically, Black has been synonymous with Ethiopian or African, most specifically sub-Saharan African. Today, we generally use Black to refer to dark skinned people of African descent.

Politically, Black is used as a symbol of oppression and resistance to racism; a theme that has been teased out in great detail by Beckford and others.[3] Beckford goes as far as to suggest that even White people can be politically Black if they engage in anti-hegemonic resistance against White oppression. The sociological and political use of Black sometimes converge in the case of some Asians who because they are not White and experience racism at the hands of racist Whites, align themselves with people of African descent as Black. Theologically, Black is used as a signifier by which to critique the human experience of racism, hence the discipline of 'Black Theology'. Here it is felt that there is a particular theological expression that emerges because of the experience of black suffering at the hands of White racists in their attempt to diminish Black humanity. As Jagessar and Reddie, the editors of a recent publication point out, "we use the term 'Black' to identify ourselves as a socially constructed 'other' when juxtaposed against the dominant Eurocentric discourses that dominate the normal picture and definition of what it means to be really 'British'."[4]

As for being churches, as distinct from being 'Black', it's worth listening to James Cone in his seminal work, 'Black Theology and Black Power'. He describes the church as a "people called into being by the power and love of God to share in his revolutionary activity for the liberation of man".[5] If we accept this definition, then it stands to reason that the church owes its raison d'etre to the alleviation of a human condition of oppression. Indeed, Cone's main charge against White Christians in America and, by extension, Europe, is that they somehow claimed to be church whilst simultaneously being condoners and perpetrators of oppression upon Black people. The Bible reminds us that you cannot serve two masters; you must make a choice. And so, church cannot both claim to serve God in holiness whilst at the same time serve Satan and his creation, racism, that denies the image of God in man.

Church then is first and foremost a people called into existence by God to glorify Him by liberating those that are bound and oppressed. "Come to me", Jesus said, "you that are weary and heavy laden and I will give you rest". Liberation is at the heart of the remit of what it means to be church and the usefulness of any suffix or prefix in addition to 'church' must be judged by the extent to which it highlights this cardinal purpose. Black Churches in America, as in Britain, emerged and became colour-coded at a time of difficulty for Black people, using the signifier 'Black' to point to their primary mission field. And both there and here they have continued to find meaning even in what could be regarded as calmer waters, racially speaking.

The people in Britain most closely associated with these churches are those and their descendants from the Caribbean who came and settled here since the post 1940s Windrush era. To Caribbean people can be added Africans of direct African heritage and Asians from Africa and Asia who have added their presence to the Black Churches. These churches are, in the main, from the Oneness and Trinitarian Pentecostal and Holiness traditions as well as from, for example, African and Asian indigenous church traditions. As Roswith Gerloff makes clear in the first in-depth analysis of these churches, there is a wide variety of historical, theological, doctrinal and denominational traditions represented.[6] Being viewed through the prism of colour can only ever be one vantage point when relating to these churches.

BUT WHY CALL THEM 'BLACK'?

I remember reading an article that has been long lost, in which the writer roundly castigated those who supported the idea of referring to churches by skin colour. It is fair to say that he believed this to be divisive, even demonic in its divisiveness. I was never sure whether the writer's problem was unease with the term 'Black' or whether he genuinely worried that if some insisted on calling themselves 'Black Church' then others may start calling themselves 'White Church' and that that polarity might lead to racial confrontation or even a race war. However one views his and other people's reasoning, it is a fair challenge to ask, 'Why call churches by colour?' Let me attempt something of a chronological response.

Back in the day from the 1950s and onwards, Christians came to Britain from those parts of the world mentioned earlier: the Caribbean, Africa and Asia. As is normal, these Black people, then as now, belonged to denominations of various types, including mainstream churches such as Roman Catholic, Anglican, Methodist, Baptist and

Reformed. They also belonged to churches such as the Seventh Day Adventists and a wide range of Church of God, Holiness and Apostolic Pentecostal churches. The experience of those early migrants, at a time when the only churches were those peopled and operated by the White indigenous population, was sobering. One historian, Adrian Hastings, makes the observation that "immigrants found the existing churches mostly staid, elderly and very little interested in them".[7] All the signs are that the reason for White disinterest was quite simply the dark pigmentation of the new migrants. Still today, colour prejudice feeds and informs the worldview of many. From early on, Black people in the post Windrush era graphically describe from personal experience the context they found in Britain: for example, their experience on the bus, when looking for rooms to rent, on the job, in education, in fact anywhere they cared to look, their reception was as cold as the winter weather they had to get accustomed to. Io Smith complains, "I was looking for love and warmth and encouragement. I believed that the first place I would find that was in the church, but it wasn't there".[8]

Not even Black Anglicans, Catholics, Methodists and Baptists could find a home amongst their White brothers and sisters, and the plight of Black Pentecostals was no better. Not that, coming from exclusivist Holiness/Pentecostal backgrounds, there were likely to be many converts to what they viewed as 'nominal mainstreamism', even if those churches were warm and welcoming. But the White existing churches could have offered a place to 'katch' or shelter for a while, whilst the newcomers worked out what to do next. The combination of a missiological desire to plant the Holiness/Pentecostal churches to which they belonged from home, coupled with the icy cold rejection from mainstream churches meant that almost as soon as the new immigrants arrived in Britain new churches began to be formed. They initially began in people's living and bed rooms, graduating to school, community and church halls, then to the acquisition of redundant, often dilapidated, church buildings. In myriad ways, these Black Christians demonstrated an intense aptitude to transplant their spiritual homes because of what Gerloff calls a "sense of mission" to their own people and to wider society.[9]

Initial White reaction to these new Black Churches was sociological, not theological. On the one hand, some thought that these people were forming their own churches because of their psychotherapeutic need for comfort in their alienation from White society. On the other hand, some saw them as divisive and militant, an inappropriate response to exclusion and oppression, engaging in a Black struggle liberation. Hastings observed however that these churches were not 'Black' in principle, only in membership.[10] Hastings probably overstates the case, but he has a point. And yet, White observers, religious and secular, viewed these churches as sociological constructs which if they had anything to do with religion at all were 'sects' not bona fide churches. The fact that all of the early Black Churches were transplants from people's homelands, sometimes with White US headquarters, escaped virtually all onlookers. They saw them as manifestations of circumstance, bastardised children of rejection, as someone, Joel Edwards I believe, puts it.

From this sociological standpoint then, analysts sought to label these pseudo churches based, not on their official denominational names or ideology, but according to the sociological phenotype of their followers. Suddenly, it mattered not what denomination you were from – New Testament Church of God, Church of God of Prophecy, Cherubim and Seraphim, Seventh Day Adventist, Shiloh Apostolic, et al.; you were from a Black Church. Bishop Wilfred Woods points out in the first Directory of these Churches in 1984 that the term 'Black-led Church' was first coined and applied by White Church leaders.[11] Indeed, when this term was first used, Black leaders rejected it, one saying, "This is not how we see ourselves".[12] All indications are that the early pioneers of these churches understood their churches as universal in missiological scope and they sought to minister so. They focussed upon establishing the churches they knew as the vehicles for rescuing their own people from the ravages of a racist society but at the same time they reached out to the wider community, often holding meetings in the markets and leafleting the neighbourhoods where they met for worship. All to no avail, as the few Whites who responded quickly went away once they found that the congregants were Black and for the most part culturally different. I have concluded that a key reason whey Black Churches have remained Black is due to the colour prejudice of Whites, Christians and non-Christians alike. What is it about the White psyche that makes it feels it cannot come under Black leadership?

Alongside the socio-political-theological discourse about Black and Church, there has been a lively parallel discourse within the Black

Church as to the legitimacy of terms like 'Black', 'Black-led', or 'Black-majority' Churches. A corresponding question was raised by the editor of the very first issue of the journal 'Black Theology in Britain' in 1998, when Emmanuel Lartey asked, "what is it about colours in theology?"[13] The first serious interrogation of this was by Arlington Trotman in 1992.[14] Trotman cited one Black Church leader, Malachi Ramsay, saying that such practice was "degrading and lacking in respect". Trotman concluded that "it would be more precise if these churches were named according to their historical and theological foundations". This is because, according to Trotman, "the Body of Christ has not been caste in colour, class or creed, but the word was made flesh for all and racial barriers were broken down in the crucifixion and resurrection". Trotman's preferred classification for the so-called Black Church, was 'Holiness-Pentecostal Church'.

The debate over the colouring of these churches was reignited recently by Mark Sturge who argued that the term 'Black Majority Church' was a "more excellent name".[15] For Sturge, Black majority focussed on the ethnicity of the majority of members rather than leaders and was an example of self-naming. It was better therefore than the Black-led term imposed by White liberals, and better also than Holiness-Pentecostal because that term had foreign roots in an unsavoury racist past. My own views, teased out in my recent book, 'Respect: Understanding Caribbean British Christianity', argues for objectivity and pragmatism.[16] The sociological, political and theological use of Black, even when applied to church, is fine when used with clear reasoning and purpose. However, what is far better is to use the names churches give themselves rather than the short-hand social classification of the use of the term 'Black' to identify them. I recognise however that without a signifier like 'Black' the liberative nature of the churches in question may not be as clear.

Are Black Churches contributing to cohesion or polarising Christians and other faith groups?

The term 'community cohesion' has been popularised by the government in recent times. This has been so particularly since the disturbances in places like Bradford, Burnley and Oldham in 2001. A report published by the government highlights their findings into the underlying factors hindering or enabling community cohesion.[17] Among the key factors identified as hindering community cohesion is that communities tend to, metaphorically, live in silos, or run along parallel lines, with the effect that different peoples' "lives often do not seem to touch at any point, let alone overlap and promote any meaningful exchanges". The report found that issues of importance in effecting and maintaining cohesion are empowerment, participation, associational activities and common purpose, supporting networks and reciprocity, collective norms and values, trust, safety and belonging. In these matters, the Home Office takes a lead, followed by the department of Communities and Local Government, but cohesion is meant to be at the heart of all departments, as the Government attempts to make a multi-faceted society, what used to be called a multi-cultural society (until Trevor Phillips told us the term was bad for us), cohere across cultures, faiths, class, gender and race/ethnicity. The report states that "community cohesion is not something that is achieved once and for all; it is an ongoing process that requires sustained commitment" at all levels. The very reason why cohesion is necessary, i.e. diversity, militates against achieving it.

I beg to suggest that the government is a 'Johnny come lately' to the cohesion debate. From the early centuries of the first millennium AD, the church was already thrashing out how you can make the concept of Trinity work. How do three persons make one God and one God three persons in a 'Blessed Trinity'? Although not all Black Churches are Trinitarian, cohesion has been a major preoccupation for all of them, though expressed differently. Almost from their point of initiation in this country these churches began to seek to work on cohesion projects. These attempts can be seen in the work of the Centre for Black and White Christian Partnership, the Zebra Project, the International Ministerial Council of Great Britain, the Afro-Westindian United Council of Churches, the African and Caribbean Evangelical Alliance, the Council of Black Led Churches and a host of other 'ecumenical' projects aiming to bring coherence to their diversity. There is a natural tension between diversity and unity and to discuss whether Black Churches have been a help or a hindrance in cohesion we may need to look at whether they have encouraged and enabled the qualities identified in the government's report mentioned above: empowerment, participation, associational activities and common purpose, supporting networks and reciprocity, collective norms and values, trust, safety and and belonging. Again, I beg to suggest that Black Churches have and do.

Black Churches and agencies have been better at relating to their own communities and churches and less adept at relating to other faiths. This is not surprising given that these churches are relatively new and preoccupied with securing their existence. The complexity of interfaith relations has almost inevitably been put on the back burner and is only in recent times receiving some attention. For example, this writer represents the Black Churches locally on the Birmingham Faith Leaders Group; the Council of Black Led Churches has a representative on the Birmingham Council of Faiths; nationally I represent the Black Majority Churches on the government's Faith Communities Consultative Council; and the Minority Ethnic Christian Affairs department of Churches Together in England has a representative from the Black Churches on the Interfaith Network. This may not as yet represent 'cohesion', but there is certainly the beginning of relationships.

To further answer this question, we need to look behind the term 'Black Church' to what more these churches do and what more they symbolise. I have already shown that Black Churches have theological and historical existences. Also I have shown that these churches did not seek to identify themselves as Black Churches, rather, they have been contextually named so and ultimately have embraced the notion of colour-coding in a racialised British context. It is worthy of note that many of these churches exist in other parts of the world where they are not colour defined. For example, can we imagine referring to the New Testament Church of God in Jamaica as a Black-led or Black-majority Church? Probably not. So, what more do these churches do and what more do they signify? Here, it's probably important to say that Black Churches in Britain are at least as significant for what they do as for what they signify.

In the social sphere of education, employment, housing, health and culture, Black Churches have performed a crucial role for Black people and increasingly for wider society. Yet, from the inside, Selwyn Arnold criticised the Black Church for over-emphasising its spiritual ministry while neglecting the socio-economic needs of its members.[18] However, it is clear that the issue is not one of the absence of social involvement, but about the depth and breadth of that involvement. One observation of hindrance to effective social engagement is that initially, at least two of the key Black Churches owed allegiances to White headquarters abroad whose programmes they ran without sufficient regard to local needs. They were caught between responding to organisational demands that were often packaged not as obedience to the church but to Christ, and responding to local social needs. This presented a dichotomy that was often not well managed. It has therefore taken time for these churches and newer expressions of them to emerge with a clearer understanding of how a radical commitment to Jesus Christ's gospel can also mean radical commitment to social justice.

To the extent that they have embraced a social gospel agenda, they have been a signifier of hope to a hard-pressed people. One Black person I spoke to recently said that although not a regular church goer, knowing that there is a Council of Black Led Churches in Birmingham makes her 'feel good'. These churches have provided culturally-sensitive spaces and places for Black people through Sunday Schools, Saturday Schools, other Education programmes like Black Boys Can; Housing Associations like Nehemiah, nurses in the Health Service and as volunteers to check people's blood pressure at luncheon clubs; and the list goes on. In the social sphere the Black pastor has emerged as a community worker, advocate and friend in an often friendless world. Holding communities together, helping them to cohere by strengthening the weak, Black pastors and many in their congregations have been the social workers that Social Services don't pay.

Politically, Black Churches are only now beginning to carve out a role for themselves. There is a good reason for this. As I have pointed out earlier, historians and sociologists, Black and White, often assume and attempt to prove in theses that the reason Black churches exist in Britain is because of racism. Based on this hypothesis, they then go on to parallel British Black Churches with US ones, which in the main emerged as a 'Freedom Movement', as is described by Gayraud Wilmore in his work 'Black Religion and Black Radicalism'.[19] However, as I have pointed out in my own work, the emergence of Black Churches in Britain was not primarily in response to racism, which was a contributory factor but not a central one. The central rationale in Britain was missiological. This mission/evangelism model lacked the political and economic radicalism of the Black American churches that had this in their DNA. British Black Churches were largely transplants from the Caribbean and later Africa, rather than the indigenous and organic ones in the US responding to Black dehumanisation by Whites. Ironically, although not built for the purpose, the experience of racism in Britain means that it is a matter of when, not if, the Black Churches will turn their attention to how political they can be. In a recent meeting between Baroness Amos and Black Church leaders, she pointedly remarked, "you don't seem to know how much political power you have". As Robert Beckford has pointed out, the Black Church in Britain needs to develop a political theology to accompany its emphasis upon mission and social engagement.[20] The signs are good, but still the Black Church in Britain is more in potential than actualisation mode, politically speaking.

Theologically, Black Churches in Britain have stuck uncritically to a mainly Pentecostal code that owes its existence to the modern non-conformist revivals that emerged in the US around the end of the 19th and the beginning of the 20th century. Again, because these were transplanted churches, they came doctrinally pre-packaged and often 'theology averse'. This is not very helpful because as Gustavo Gutierrez suggests, theology is "the critical reflection on praxis in the light of the Word of God".[21] And, as previously indicated, James Cone insists, a church without theologians is likely to fall prey of extremisms and shortcomings due to the paucity of reflection on its life in light of the Word of God and its social, economic and political context. As I indicated earlier, in recent years a Black Theology has began to be articulated in Britain, particularly through the Journal of Black Theology. Its main drivers are not however from the traditional Black Church, but are Black Christians from mainstream churches. Clearly then, the Black Church in Britain has much more to do, particularly in the political and theological spheres if it is to reach its potential for good.

The answer to our question is not therefore a simple case of black or white, yes or no; it's much more complex than that. On a positive note, these churches have provided a space for Black people to develop their complex identity and feel included in a country where they often are excluded and to be in a majority when their day-to-day experience is of being a minority. They have provided nurture and confidence building space: coaching, mentoring and role modelling by Black people for Black people. 'Black' has provided a motif for cultural and even spiritual identity where multiple denominational rivalries might have prevailed. It has spiritually fed, educated, empowered and raised

Black people's self-esteem, and as Yvonne Channor has shown from her work in Sheffield, Black youngsters brought up in church behave better and do better educationally and professionally. Black Churches have demonstrated to the Church of England, for example, and other mainstream churches that Black people are not leadership averse. In these and myriad other ways, Black Churches have been a force for good and made their contribution to church and community cohesion.

There is however, a downside to Black Church existence in Britain which may deter cohesion. It could be argued that there is present what someone calls 'colonial baggage'.[22] This sense of looking elsewhere for legitimisation, for authentication and for direction, which is rooted in the origins of the Black Churches in Britain has led to a degree of passivity in key areas, stymieing self development and self understanding. Whilst Black Churches have done well in addressing the social needs of their constituency and even wider community, they have not been as effective in challenging the political root causes of these social ills. Ecclesiologically, it may well be the case that some would-be partners fail to look beyond the colour coding of these churches to the social, spiritual, economic and political areas of commonness and partnership. However, until Black Churches liberate themselves from their inhibitions in the political and theological areas of their existence and sharply focus on their context, their contribution to cohesion will have an unnecessary deficit. This has been argued since the 1970s by such as Ira Brooks of the New Testament Church of God.[23]

CONCLUSION

It is not my belief that Black Churches polarise other Christians, churches and faiths. Rather, by their presence they provide clear points of cultural and sociological, political and theological engagement. Concluding where I started, the fact that these churches have 'grown' several of us who now occupy important positions in the world of ecumenical and interfaith affairs, and who regularly liaise with government and other key aspects of British society is evidence of a significant contribution to cohesion and the building of greater understanding and mutual regard. As Black Churches develop theologically, politically and socially, I believe they will become an even greater force for good. And who knows, maybe one day these churches will be as well known for their other virtues in at least equal measure as they are known for their identity as Black Churches. Dare we, in the spirit of Martin Luther King Jr, dream of such a day? I do.

A talk delivered at Birmingham University, June 2007

1. R Beckford, Dread and Pentecostal, SPCK 2000, p.5
2. Richard Reddie, Abolition, Lion Hudson, 2007, p.16
3. Beckford, Dread and Pentecostalism
4. Miahael Jagessar & Anthony Reddie eds., Postcolonial Black British Theology, Peterborough: Epworth, 2007, pxiii
5. James Cone, Black Theology and Black Power, Harper and Row, 1969, p.63
6. Roswith Gerloff, A Plea for British Black Theologies, Peter Lang, 1992, p.51
7. Adrian Hastings, A History of English Christianity 1920-1990, SCM Press1991, p.559
8. Io Smith, An Ebony Cross, Marshall Morgan and Scott, 1989, p.40
9. Gerloff, p23
10. Hastings, p621
11. Wilfred Woods in AWUCOC Directory, 1984.
12. Gerloff
13. Emmanuel Lartey ed, Black theology in Britain, issue 1, 1998, p7
14. rlington Trotman, Black, Black-led, or what? In Joel Edwards ed., Lets Praise Him Again, Eastbourne: Kingsway, p12-35
15. Mark Sturge, Look what the Lord has done, Milton Keynes: Scripture Union
16. Joe Aldred, Respect, 2006
17. Community Cohesion: A report of the independent review team chaired by Ted Cantle. http://image.guardian.co.uk/sys-files/Guardian/documents/2001/12/11/communitycohesionreport.pdf
18. Selwyn Arnold, From Scepticism to Hope, Grove Books, 1992, p53
19. Gayraud Wilmore, Black Religion and Black Radicalism, New York: Orbis, p74
20. Beckford, Dread and Pentecostalism
21. Gustavo Gutierrez, The Power of the Poor in History, London: SCM Press, 1983, pvii
22. Maxine Howell-Baker and Tonya Bolton, Am I my brothers and sisters keeper?, Christian Aid
23. Ira Brooks, Another gentleman to the ministry

CHAPTER 10

The Windrush – mission and the aftermath

INTRODUCTION

'The Windrush' stands as an enduring icon of post-Second World War migration and modern multiculturalism in Britain. This diesel-powered motor ship, originally known as The Monte Rosa, was first launched on 4 December 1930 in Hamburg. It was initially used as a cruise ship. Many of its passengers were privileged Nazi Party members, enjoying the party's 'Strength through Joy' programme. During the Second World War the Monte Rosa doubled as barracks for German troops and as a prisoner transport ship. For example, it was used in the deportation of Jews from Norway to concentration camps and prisons.

The Monte Rosa was captured by Britain in 1945, held as a war prize, and was renamed the S S Empire Windrush in 1947. Named after the 'River Windrush', 'Empire' was one of a series of second-hand ships re-named after British rivers. The Empire Wansbeck is another, named after the River Wansbeck. Britain used the Empire Windrush principally as a troopship on voyages from Southampton to Sri Lanka, Singapore, Hong Kong, Japan, et al. But she eventually met her end sunk in the Mediterranean Sea in 1954 after a catastrophic fire in her engine room. Four members of the crew were killed in the explosion and fire, but miraculously, all 1276 passengers were saved.

In the middle of all this, the ship sailed from Australia via the Atlantic to England and stopped off in Kingston, Jamaica. While there, news spread that anyone who could afford it, could sail to England. Some 492 passengers took up the offer and joined 60 Polish women on board, who had become displaced during the Second World War. Also boarding in Kingston were Trinidadian calypsonians Lord Kitchener and Lord Beginner. There was even a stowaway, 25-year-old Avrill Wanchove, a Jamaican seamstress, who was discovered seven days into the journey. The good-natured passengers and crew had a whip-round for her, raising £50 which paid her fare and gave her £4 pocket money!

The SS Empire Windrush landed at Tilbury Docks on 22 June 1948 and the British Parliament immediately began discussing immigration controls before eventually allowing the passengers to disembark. This, the largest group of Caribbean migrants to arrive at the same time, seem to send shockwaves through the British establishment.

How noteworthy that this ship with such a complex history was the vehicle of this seminal human cargo that has come to so symbolise the aspirations of a people. That the SS Empire Windrush eventually sank but its cargo was saved may also speak something about the mission and destiny of the Black Church Movement in Britain. Although there were Caribbean people here before the Windrush, this iconic landing heralded the start of what is called the Windrush Generation.

The ensuing migration into Britain is well documented, but has become enmeshed in clichés and stereotypes, such as everybody from the Caribbean becoming assumed Jamaicans, and the African continent is often collapsed into the Nigerianisation or the Ghananisation of Africa. Migrants have come from various (mostly) English speaking parts of the Caribbean, numerically led by Jamaicans and Barbadians, and from across Africa, led by Nigerians and Ghanaians. According to the 2001 census, there are about one million African and Caribbean people in Britain, making up approximately 2% of the British population; in addition there may be another one million of mixed African or Caribbean heritages. Demographically, over 90% of the Windrush Generation live in England and approximately 70% live in London, followed by the West Midlands and other major conurbations or 'inner cities'.

THE BLACK CHURCH MOVEMENT

The Black Church Movement in Britain stands as probably the most distinctive feature of the Windrush Generation. I am aware that for some people, talk of 'Black Church', Black-led Church, Black-majority Church, Black Church Movement, Black Christian Movement is somewhat uncomfortable. For some these are racist, divisive or at best unhelpful terms. For me, these are primarily descriptive sociological terminologies. They have socio-cultural, spiritual, economic and political ramifications too. There can be something determinative and self-fulfilling about descriptive terms, however, for academic, theological and even missiological reasons, these terms help to identify who and what we are talking about.

With reference to terminologies, the 'Black Christian Movement' refers to the phenomenon in Britain of Black Christians across the denominational spectrum. The 'Black Church Movement' sits within the 'Black Christian Movement' as those churches initiated and operated by people of African and Caribbean descent. We call these Black-led or Black-majority churches even though the real picture is more complex. Is a church a Black-led Church if it has its roots in White America, for example? Or is it a Black-majority Church if it is an inner city Anglican, Catholic, Methodist, Baptist, United Reformed Church, Elim or Assemblies of God Church? Discuss.

However we choose to define them, Black Church networks and independent fellowships have been gaining strength since their inception in the early 1950s. These churches exist mainly in major urban conurbations in England, but have spread to Wales, Scotland, and Ireland. In spite of their being a small percentage of British society (2-3.5%), African and Caribbean people disproportionately prop up falling national church attendance. According to recent research, 48% of Black people attend church regularly; three times the rate of the White community (Churchgoing in the UK, Tear Fund 2007).

It is a popular assumption that Black equals Pentecostal when it comes to Black Christianity in Britain. However, statistically, there are more Black Christians in the historic or mainstream churches in Britain than traditional Black Pentecostal ones. Pentecostals account for 23% of Black Christian churchgoers, Roman Catholics 23% and the Church of England 19% (Tear Fund). When we add other historic churches like Methodist, Baptist and the URC, it is clear that overwhelmingly Black people in Britain are non-Pentecostals. Amazingly, the people who arrived in Britain to face signs stating, "No Irish, no dogs, no blacks" and who were initially rejected by the host churches, now populate the entire spectrum of Christian denominations in Britain. Every Sunday there are approximately half to one million Black people attending a church service somewhere.

Black Christians in Britain have come a long way since the early days of the Windrush era. Then, with evangelistic zeal, they established fellowships in living rooms, attics, school and church halls, before moving on to build or purchase the prestigious stock of properties we now associate with Black Churches.

Initially, Black Christians and their churches were preoccupied with personal and organisational survival, but increasingly they have become socially, economically and politically mature and active beyond their immediate membership. Black Christians in this post-Windrush era are ministers of churches of all denominations, key leaders of large organisations, politicians, consultants, educators and much besides. They have not yet reached the 'promised land', but the pioneers of the Windrush era could not have envisaged that the little acorns they planted in prayer meetings and in their resistance to racism in historic/ mainstream churches would have yielded the Black Christian Movement of today. And to think they only came for 'five years' to earn some corn and return home to feed the chicks for a better life.

I sense though that the greater mission is ahead of the Windrush Generation. But if successful mission is to be done in the future, a greater understanding of its context needs to be developed. There is a temptation to go into all the world as a first step, but I am firmly of the view that starting at the known, at Jerusalem, is a sound, even biblical, principle. Ethnically speaking, Jerusalem for the Black Christian community is the Black and Minority Ethnic (BME) communities. And we have some identity issues that must be grappled with before, or even as, we seek to impact the wider society. So, let us talk about identity.

I am currently reading Vivian Green's 'A New History of Christianity', and in it he states that according to European mythological religious beliefs, the devil sometimes took the form of, among other things, a spider or a black pig. Green continues, "Satan was more often depicted as a monstrous human being with bestial characteristics, 'like', as a monk of Cluny said, 'a small black Ethiopian horribly deformed, with horns coming out of his ears, and fire from his mouth as if he was about to eat the very flesh of the sick monk'". Mythologically, black is a grotesque object of fear. No wonder in western culture many Black people in our eagerness to get along, quickly want to move on from self-identity to enmeshing ourselves into the identities of other groups, because, we say, colour doesn't matter. I am tempted to say if it didn't matter, God wouldn't have created it. I am firmly of the belief that many Black people have imbibed the western pseudo-scientific inferiorisation of Blackness and are in hiding from our skin colour. Except, of course if you are in the black at the bank.

To speak of Black people in the world is all right for many. But to apply 'Black' to 'church' throws up real challenges for them. Here, Black Church, Black-led Church, Black-majority Church, Black Church Movement, Black Christianity, etc., can be viewed as unacceptable terms. Recently, my friend Nims Obunge (of the Peace Alliance, Peace Week, etc) speaking on BBC Radio 4 Sunday Programme robustly rejected the concept of Black Churches, intimating that he viewed the term as divisive and therefore injurious to racial harmony. Years ago in the work of Roswith Gerloff on the Black Church Movement in Britain, one Black Pentecostal objected to the term and its connotation, "that is not the way we see ourselves", he retorted. And in an anthology edited by Joel Edwards in the 1990s, Arlington Trotman wrote a chapter titled, 'Black, Black-led or what?' in which he critiqued the use of Black in relation to church. Trotman rejected the use of the Black as an ethnic typology in describing churches in favour of theologically symbolic terms like Holiness and Pentecostal. This theme was revisited in 2005 by Mark Sturge, then of the African and Caribbean Evangelical Alliance, in which he affirmed the use of Black provided it was not the then popular 'Black-led', which he regarded as externally imposed. Sturge favoured the 'more excellent name' Black majority Churches, which has become common currency since. I tend to use these terms Black-led, Black-majority Church, interchangedly as is appropriate for the context. But what precisely will the Black Church do with its Blackness? Discuss.

WINDRUSH GENERATION AND MISSIOLOGICAL ISSUES

However it describes itself, the Caribbean led church has declined over the past fifteen to twenty years. It is still functional but many of its brightest people have migrated outwards into the wider church and it has not found a way of holding on to sufficient numbers of its young professionals, and young people in general. It does not sufficiently engage with mainstream society for mission and has not forged strong working relationships with its African brothers and sisters. Yet, the

Caribbean churches have spawned excellent social projects in housing, education and prison work among other sectors.

There is a very noisy debate within the wider British Caribbean community about its lack of progress over the past sixty years since the landing of the Windrush. Like few other minority ethnic groups, African Caribbean people find themselves profiled badly in all but a very few social indicators: single gender head of households, absent fathers, teenage parenting, prison population, underachievement in education, unemployment, absent from the business world, politics, health, not to mention a prevalence in gangs, drugs, guns and knife use. It does not help that many of the community's activists tend to blame these shortcomings on the twin-headed monster of racism and the Asians who are deemed to be more powerful economically and politically.

In this navel-gazing exercise, little is made of the successes gained, particularly in sports, music and popular culture where if Richard Dawkins is correct, Jamaican patois has become the new lingua franca in urban Britain. Today's context is contingent upon a history of non-belonging, temporary mindset, societal exclusion, racism and a failure to change tact once plan A did not work. An expression of this cultural 'outside looking in' status is an intense clinging to the identity of 'African Caribbean' which speaks of a past heritage while saying nothing of present belonging.

I believe the Windrush Generation has two significant missiological hurdles to scale: Caribbean/African relations, and Black churches/historic churches relations. Put simply, none of us on our own is church. It takes us all to be the church of Jesus Christ. I believe our faith offers us a template for engagement with those with whom we have had a troubled history. Such engagement should be undergirded by a sound theological philosophy of oneness: One God, one humanity, one Christian faith. Often, in attempting to construct relationships we speedily move to actions. And sometimes action is important. But if our relationship is to progress it must be built less on what we do with, to and for each other and based more on what and who we are to and for one another. Less doing, more being. Our tendency therefore 'to do' can sometimes lead to empty and meaningless actions. At the heart of our relationship, I believe, must be an understanding that there is one Creator and Sustainer, in whose image and likeness we are all created; that we are therefore brothers and sisters in humanity and now in the church, in which Jesus Christ is spiritual head and we members one of another. I believe this is what is had in mind in Jesus' words that the world will believe because of our love for one another. A love that is a heart condition, a soul condition, a mind condition. When our love for one another is the real cause of our action, and when we have taken time to know what it's like to walk a mile in our brother or sister's shoes, only then are we truly ready to have dealings with those who are the 'other'.

The SS Empire Windrush in its multiple identities and uses, even in its sinking, reminds us that we need to be ready to sacrifice the shell of our existence in favour of the souls of men and women. It may yet be that the Windrush Generation values the carrier of mission more than those to whom we were sent. True mission starts as Jonah discovered when we take the message of salvation to those to whom we were sent.

A presentation delivered at Redeemed Christian Church of God's Evangelism and Missions Week, London 10 March 2012

CHAPTER 11

Christians as salt and light in the world (based on Matthew 5.13-16)

(13)You are the salt of the earth. But if the salt loses its saltiness, how can it be made salty again? It is no longer good for anything, except to be thrown down and trampled by men.
(14) You are the light of the world. A city on a hill cannot be hidden.
(15) Neither do people light a lamp and put it under a bowl. Instead they put it on its stand, and it gives light to everyone in the house.
(16) In the same way, let your light shine before men, that they may see your good deeds and praise your Father in heaven.

Today, I want to reflect upon Jesus' words to us concerning the Christian qualities as salt and light in the world.

1. What do salt and light mean?
2. How the Windrush people have fared as salt and light in Britain
3. Present and future generations of Caribbean heritage people being salt and light

THE CONTEXT OF THIS TEXT

According to R T France in the Tyndale New Testament Commentary on Matthew, this text falls within what Matthew's gospel regards as Jesus' main period of public ministry; beginning from his first appearance as a preacher and extending to his disciples' recognition of his unique status and mission (Matthew 4.17-16.20). The text we are looking at comes from the section of chapters 5-7 that is commonly referred to as the 'Sermon on the Mount'. It is probably worth pointing out that what appears here as one sermon, appears also in different renderings in Mark (e.g. chapter 9) and Luke (e.g. chapter 6.20-49), which suggests that these are a collection of Jesus' teachings rather than a single sermon delivered once.

According to France, this account by Matthew deals with the character, duties, attitudes and dangers of the Christian life in the kingdom of heaven. In verses 13-16 of chapter 5 we find Jesus utilising the imagery of salt and light to make the point.

SALT

Salt can be said to possess two essential uses: to give flavour and prevent corruption. The Oxford Dictionary defines salt as, "sodium chloride, a white crystalline substance which gives seawater its characteristic taste and is used for seasoning or preserving food". In popular parlance, we speak of:

'Rubbing salt into the wound': meaning to make a painful experience even more painful;
'The salt of the earth': meaning someone of goodness and strength of character;
'Worth one's salt': meaning good and competent at one's job or allotted task;
'Take something with a pinch of salt': meaning to regard something said as exaggerated;
'Sit below the salt': meaning to be of lower social standing.

All of these sayings convey the sense in which salt is deemed to be virtuous as flavour and preservative. We can interpret Jesus' teaching therefore to mean that the disciples' mission is to make the earth a purer and more palatable place. But they will only do so as they retain their distinctive character, because unsalty salt is of no value.

But, can salt lose its saltiness? Sources tell me that pure salt cannot lose its saltiness. However, it is thought that impure salt can gradually become unsalty as the sodium chloride dissolves. It may be more helpful to make a distinction between salt that has been fully formed and salt that has not. Ralph Gower in 'Manners and Customs of Bible Times' says that when salt was collected from the Dead Sea area, some of it was good salt while some of it was not. The salt that was not properly salty was not thrown away but was stored in the Jerusalem Temple, and when the winter rains made the marble courtyards slippery, the unsalty salt was spread on them to make the marble less slippery. Hence Jesus' saying that the salt that has lost its saltiness will be trodden underfoot of men.

In the Greek world from which our New Testament comes, the concept of an absence of taste, or loss of taste, was synonymous with being, or becoming, foolish. We are told that the Jewish Rabbis commonly used salt as an image of wisdom. We see this in Paul's writing in Colossians 4.6, "Let your conversation be always full of grace, seasoned with salt, so that you may know how to answer everyone". In other words, an unsalty disciple that lacks the ability to season, add taste and preserve is a foolish disciple who has no influence in the world. Again, we are told that in Jewish eating custom, salt had a particular function as a symbol of peace. Thus to 'eat salt' was to be at peace; in fact the whole meal was symbolic that peace reigned. We see this link established in Mark's account of the words of Jesus in the Sermon on the Mount: "Have salt in yourselves, and be at peace with each other" (Mark 9.50).

LIGHT

Like salt, light affects its environment. The Oxford dictionary says that light is the natural agent that stimulates sight and makes things visible. We refer to light in other guises too, we speak of:

> 'Someone's eyes lighting up': implying excitement and joy;
> 'Something coming to light': meaning to become known, or evident;
> 'Going out like a light': meaning to fall asleep or become unconscious suddenly;
> 'Light at the end of the tunnel': meaning that a period of difficulty is ending, there is hope;
> 'Seen the light': meaning to undergo conversion.

These all indicate light as the source of illumination. In our modern Britain we take light for granted. At night, we walk into our houses and the first thing we do is switch on the light. Just occasionally we are inconvenienced by a power-cut. But some of us know what it is like not to have light at our fingertips. We know what it means to have to feel around in the dark or in inadequate light, because of the total absence of light, or because of inadequate lighting. I still have memories of being a boy in deep rural Jamaica, walking on stone-paved roads without streetlights. I lost the odd toe-nail because I did not see the stone in the road, got poked by the tree branch, walked into the odd low lying wall – all in the dark. There always appeared to be more 'duppies' in the darkness. I cannot tell you of the number of people who first spoke in tongues because of sensations that were induced by the dark. The need for light is unquestioned, both when applied to natural and to inner illumination. Ignorance has caused no end of difficulties in our world.

Light is of little use when located in some obscure corner and covered over. Generally speaking the higher the light source, the better. This is why we site our bulbs in the ceiling or high on the walls in our homes. This is why you and I are not meant to be going around with our heads held low, or underestimating our contributions. We were never intended to be people who lie low. As Nelson Mandela suggests, our playing small does not become us as the people of God. Referring to the oil lamp that was used at that time, and with which some of us will be familiar, Jesus says that people do not light a lamp and cover it under a bowl; they put it on a stand so that all in the house can benefit from its illumination. The text links the disciples' light to what s/he does: let your deeds be such that they lead people to glorify the God that gives you so much power for good.

I find it significant that the text says, "You are the salt of the earth" and "You are the light of the world". Not that you are going to be, but "you are". This state of being is one that I wish to emphasise today. It links up with several other texts that tell us: "now are we the sons of God"; "as many as are led by the Spirit of God are the sons of God"; Jesus said to the dying thief on the cross, "today you will be with me in paradise." I cannot speak for you, but I am personally fed up with Christians who attempt to subvert this God-given state of well-being by calling Christians back to first works over and over and over again: at every weekly service, every seminar, every retreat, etc. If you have committed your life to God, you are, not going to be, already salt, light, a city on a hill! Stop undermining your status, stop doubting the work God has already done in you, and don't let any one, however powerful they may appear, undermine your status in God as a full son or daughter! You are a star, no matter what anybody says about you. As Paul in his letter to the Philippians says:

Therefore my dear friends, as you have always obeyed, not only in my presence, but now much more in my absence, continue to work out your salvation with fear and trembling, for it is God who works in you to will and to act according to his good purpose. Do everything without complaining or arguing, so that you may become blameless and pure, children of God without fault in a crooked and depraved generation, in which you shine like stars in the universe as you hold out the word of life...(2.12-16).

HOW THE WINDRUSH PEOPLE HAVE FARED AS SALT AND LIGHT IN BRITAIN

In this season when you are celebrating the Caribbean, it is only fitting that I should say something about how some Caribbean people have exemplified what it means to be salt and light here in Britain. The exploits of Caribbean Christian people are of course too extensive for me to attempt to catalogue them here, if indeed I could. So let me restrict myself to a few words about those who came to Britain from the Caribbean in what I am calling the Windrush era, i.e. since the mid 1940s.

Let me preface what I will say here by stating that I am not much into self-deprecation. To the extent that I cannot even agree with Andre Crouch when he sings so beautifully and movingly, “I don’t know why Jesus loves me”. I can give you a lot of reasons why Jesus loves you and me. You and I are made in his image; we bear his stamp of ownership; his breath is in us; we are the apex of his creation. That is why, like the woman who lost her coin and the shepherd who lost his sheep, God is ever prepared to seek us out until he finds us. However, we humans may view each other, our humanity is precious to God!

The people who came from the Caribbean from the mid-1940s onwards were not, generally speaking, from the upper echelons of Caribbean societies. Of course there are some exceptions, but I think you can rest assured that as the majority of jobs for which people came were menial; there would not have been too many brain surgeons applying to drive London and Birmingham buses, to work as nursing auxiliaries or to work in clothes mills and coal mines. The majority were economic migrants from lower down the social order, many of whom had to borrow money or sell family animals to raise the fare to travel to Britain. It is fascinating to note that the people who started the Black Church Movement in Britain were from such humble beginnings. Of them it can surely be said,

> Think of what you were when you were called. Not many of you were wise by human standards; not many were influential; not many were of noble birth. But God chose the foolish things of the world to shame the wise; God chose the weak things of the world to shame the strong. He chose the lowly things of this world and the despised things and the things that are not to nullify the things that are, so that no one may boast before him (1 Corinthians 1.26-29).

The conditions these people endured are astonishing to recall. We sometimes forget that these were young people, often separated from their loved ones: spouses, children, family and friendship networks. They had to tolerate repeated rejection in trying to find accommodation and jobs. They faced signs like, 'No dogs, No Irish, No niggers'. One records that landlords repeatedly told him, "I would love to rent you the room, but my neighbours won't like it". He concluded that if only he could find the neighbour, then he would sort things out. Alas, this was everybody's excuse. Then when they did find a room, many had to share the beds, sometimes sleeping by shifts.

The testimonies of being frozen out of the White-led churches are well known. Some who belonged to mainstream churches from home are until this day fighting to become accepted as equal partners in their churches. Pentecostals, Holiness and other traditions brought over from the Caribbean, for years were called 'sects' and 'cults'. When they tried to hire the use of existing church buildings they were either refused or relegated to the church hall at awkward times. When they rented school halls, the caretaker would invariably refuse to clean the place and instead operated as a key rattler, pushing them out on time irrespective of what was happening. They often had to bring their own disinfectant and broom to clean up the mess left behind from the party the night before. Trying to buy buildings usually meant ending up with the dilapidated leftovers of the mainstream churches. Thousands of pounds having to be spent on perennial repairs. So lowly were they that when my predecessors at the Centre for Black and White Christian Partnership wanted to establish a theological training course for Black pastors they had to argue for special dispensation from the university of Birmingham: without this they would not have been able to study at university level. Professor Walter Hollenweger says of them: "Christians in Britain prayed for revival, but did not recognise it when it came, because it was Black".

But in the midst of all this and more, these remarkable pioneers have managed to give us an identity that cannot be ignored by anyone from the top of government to persons in the street. If it were not for Black people, today some of Britain's inner cities would be practically without a Christian witness. Here in Birmingham, we are courted by civic, political and religious powers alike. I am reminded of my biblical namesake, Joseph, who went to Egypt as a slave and rose to become second in command. I am not suggesting that we have now reached the Promised Land, but I am certainly saying 'Look where God has brought us, He has brought us from a mighty long way!' I am saying that in their different ways, our pioneering fathers and mothers found ways of letting their light shine in Britain; they have been salt in a tasteless society. Now, my challenge to you is that it is your turn.

PRESENT AND FUTURE GENERATIONS OF CARIBBEAN HERITAGE PEOPLE BEING SALT AND LIGHT

You are now part of a much smarter, academically and intellectually qualified, and well-connected generation. You can get caught up in analysing where those who have gone before went wrong, or you can more profitably work out how you can shine like stars in your environment: bringing illumination, clarity, honesty and righteousness and as salt, bringing taste, preservation and penetration. It is not difficult to see where these qualities are needed.

IN THE POLITICAL ARENA

Our country is crying out for politicians possessing the qualities of salt and light: translated as integrity, honesty and justice. There are of course some Christian politicians, but at local and national levels we need more Christian influence. As a disciple of Jesus Christ, nothing is out of your reach. And politics do not only mean party politics. 'Politic' means, 'sensible, prudent and judicious'. So to be involved in politics is to be involved in the struggle for the prevalence of sensible, prudent and judicious policies. It is a struggle against the irrational, imprudent and injudicious.

IN THE SOCIAL ARENA

We need Christians involved in policy making and the outworking of how our society is organised. Christians must be at the very heart of our society if this is to be a just society. In education, housing, employment, policing, health, criminal justice, popular culture and other areas, we must not be onlookers, but salt and light.

IN THE RELIGIOUS ARENA

At a time when Christianity is divided among itself, we need people who do not only know their own tradition but who can straddle the manmade lines of divisions. We need those who can become reconcilers, not only within the Christian faith but also with people of other faiths. We need more theologians who are willing to challenge what Christians and churches believe and teach. We need more apostles, prophets, evangelists, deacons, pastors, teachers and just good Christians.

IN THE ECONOMIC ARENA

Some of you here are called to be successful business people, to employ others, to show that honesty can pay. Some of you are too comfortable in lowly paid jobs when you have the ability to excel. You need to challenge yourself to go higher. Some of you need to move up and move out.

CONCLUSION

I want to close by inviting you to join hands with the person next to you and to pray for whoever is on either side of you. If you do not know the two people to your immediate left and right, take a moment to share names. Then please pray that they will be effective as salt and light in the community: at home, school, work, church. Amen!

This sermon was preached as guest speaker at a local church service in Birmingham

Part 4

PROGRESS

CHAPTER 12

Together we can

I am writing this article sitting at a table at stand 103 of the Respect Foundation at the Wembley Live Black History Month event that is taking place at Wembley Stadium (Saturday 1 to Sunday 2 October 2011). By way of explanation, the Respect Foundation is an unregistered organisation based on the central idea from my PhD thesis that was published in 2005 as a book titled, 'Respect: Understanding Caribbean British Christianity'. The Respect Foundation seeks to encourage understanding of the 'self' and the 'other' as a means towards community cohesion. 'Respect' reasons that only as we get to know who we and others are can the task of cohering as one humanity truly begin. At a higher level, knowledge of the 'other' includes knowledge of faith in God, without whom I believe nothing exists. The Wembley Live event is sponsored by the Black History Month organisation, which is led by the irrepressible Mia Morris OBE. In addition to marking Black History Month in October with ambitious events like Wembley Live, Ms Morris publishes a regular magazine which can be seen at *www.black-history-month.co.uk*.

Having endured so much negativity recently resulting from the August (2011) disturbances, blamed by many primarily on African Caribbean British youths – even though it is now clear that participation was spread across ethnic groups, it is highly therapeutic to be reintroduced at Wembley Live to some of the greats of Black history like Pan-Africanist George Padmore; and be introduced to some enterprising new developments in the Black British community. These vary from young and emerging writers of children's books about Egyptology to health programmes that address diabetes. Walking from stand to stand I am struck by the magnanimity of pretty much everyone. There is free curry patties and expensive art. Earlier, entrepreneur Levi Roots strutted his stuff on stage, followed by the engaging vibes of the London Community Gospel Choir and Birmingham's own emerging operatic superstar Abigail Kelly. There is so much here to cheer the spirit!

As the end of my time at Wembley Live draws near my mind turns from history to the future. I am reminded of an event only a few days ago in Birmingham at the Drum Arts Centre, held to mark the start of Black History Month. There the keynote speaker Dr Hakim Adi reminded us that reading history is one thing, making history is quite another. He argued that we should not be content to read history, important as that is, especially if this leads us to put on an unreachable pedestal those we read about. I learned from Dr Adi that it is history that makes people great, not that great people make history – a lovely turn of phrase! It is ordinary people who by their actions make history! This was a timely rebuke to the post-Obama US presidency chatter that has tended to raise expectation of the need for a Black Messiah; the Black British equivalent of a Martin Luther King, Malcolm X, Nelson Mandela, or a Barack Obama. History made them great too.

I would not wish to minimise the feats of these and other individuals, or their contributions to history and contemporary life, but close examination tends to show that messianic expectations and claims are often romanticised or exaggerated. Since it is ordinary folks who do ordinary things that history makes extraordinary, I want to make brief reference to a development that I believe may mark the present time as a history making moment. The development to which I refer is epitomised by the spirit of this Wembley Live event. After years of the political activist failing to lead us into the Promised Land of prosperity and human fulfilment in Britain, I am seeing signs that as a community, African and Caribbean British people may now be serious about working together. I sense that the ordinary Black person in Britain realises that we can build on our history in this country for a better future. I do not share the view that we have achieved nothing in Britain since the Windrush. Far from it!

From an almost standing start, a near-monocultural working class community has transformed itself into an increasingly complex and trend-setting community, impacting popular culture, politics, the church and increasingly business as evidenced by exhibitors at the Wembley Live expo. One of the things we lack however is that cohesion that comes when we move away from what Marcus Garvey called the 'crab in the barrel' spirit, and instead work together. And yet, I cannot refer to 'crab in the barrel' without mentioning the historic Jamaican money-saving plan the 'pardna'. It indicates a spirit of cooperation that is in direct contradistinction to that 'crab in the barrel' metaphor. That we are stronger together, weaker apart is re-emerging as a popular philosophy among African and Caribbean people in Britain, and I welcome the new dawn.

The new or renewed spirit of cooperation I refer to here can be seen in at least two new initiatives. First, in Birmingham the emergence of United in Building Legacy (UBL) which is seeking to cohere the Black Caribbean and African community around seven core areas of justice, education (including youth and family), enterprise, faith, well-being, politics and regeneration. If Brummies of African and Caribbean heritage can truly speak and act together in these areas they may succeed in leaving a legacy of cooperation, economic and political power and influence as yet unrealised, and which many believe to be beyond us. A second development that excites me is the attempt by some of us to establish the National Church Leaders Forum (NCLF) as a voice for Black Christians in Britain. It is a common belief that the Black community and especially the 'Black Church' in Britain is organisation-rich, but due to extensive diversity, some may even say fragmentation, it lacks spiritual, missiological, political and economic synergy. In a phrase, we lack an authentic national framework and voice.

As with the Birmingham endeavour, if this national Black Christian instrument works it could make a significant difference now and leave both a legacy of spiritual potency and a prophetic voice in this nation that are not easily ignored. Maybe in years to come when future generations read history, they will read of UBL and the NCLF, regard them as catalysts for unity and view those who created them as history makers. Together we can!

This article was first published in The Vine Magazine, January 4, 2012

CHAPTER 13

Confronting challenges

1 SAMUEL 17.45-46

David said to the Philistine, "you come against me with sword and spear and javelin, but I come against you in the name of the Lord Almighty, the God of the armies of Israel, whom you have defied. This day the Lord will hand you over to me, and I'll strike you down and cut off your head. Today I will give the carcases of the Philistine army to the birds of the air, and the beasts of the earth, and the whole world will know that there is a God in Israel."

INTRODUCTION

This historic encounter between David and Goliath offers us an insightful model for study, and an inspired example of how we also might successfully handle the big challenges we inevitably face in our personal and corporate lives. Today I invite you to study with me, be inspired with me as together we reflect upon this epic story that has come down to us through the ages. By way of a definition, the word 'challenge' implies an invitation, a summon to take part in a contest (Collins English Dictionary). Think if you will of the challenge involved in a boxing match when one boxer throws down the gauntlet to the other – a fight follows. A challenge is never passive or inconsequential; there are always consequences. We fail to respond at our peril. Our lives comprise a series of contests, challenges, and how we respond to them determine the quality of our existence. So, in the face of life's challenges, are you a winner or a loser, a fighter or a quitter?

Today, with the David/Goliath encounter as our catalyst, I want to deal with my topic under five main headings: understanding the nature or character of the challenges we face; the significance or implications of the challenges we face; the preparation needed for the challenges we face; the courage to actualise victory over the challenges we face; identifying the greatest challenge we face today.

But before dealing with these five themes, allow me to make two key statements. First, today's victory almost always has its roots in yesterday's decisions and actions; there is scarcely ever such a thing as overnight success. Second, one of the key lessons we learn from Jesus is his commitment to building ordinary people into giants. Eleven of his twelve scared and denying followers became the foundation upon which the church has been built.

UNDERSTANDING THE NATURE/CHARACTER OF THE CHALLENGES WE FACE

A key to success is understanding the nature or character of the challenges we face. Jesus asked this rhetorical question in Luke 14.28, 31, "Suppose one of you wants to build a tower. Will he not first sit down and estimate the cost to see if he has enough money to complete it? Or suppose a king is about to go to war against another king. Will he not first sit down and consider whether he is able with ten thousand men to oppose the one coming against him with twenty thousand?" The answer in both cases is undoubtedly, 'yes'. As we Jamaicans say, "Yu hafi count de cast before you mount de harse". And one might say it is not always possible to do that. What if it's an emergency? In reality, most of our 'emergency' challenges can be seen from a mile off. The problem is not necessarily that things come upon us suddenly; it is that we fail to prepare. But we must take time to study and understand our challenges. We should be like the 'men of Issachar, who understood the times and knew what Israel should do' (1 Chronicles 12.32). How do we think they managed that? Did they get up one morning and understand everything? Maybe. But it's much more likely that, like the wise men who knew to follow the star that led them to Jesus, the Issacharians spent time studying to gain a mastery, an understanding of these things. The Wisdom Literature tells us, "Wisdom is supreme, therefore get wisdom. Though it cost all you have, get understanding, esteem her, and she will exalt you" (Proverbs 4.7, 8).

We note that Goliath was part of an army; he was not a loner. That army was a tenacious unit; they had pride and if they ran away, it was only to return to fight another day. Commentators note that the battle reported in our text was not being waged in the central Judean hills, because the Israeli army had chased the Philistines westwards, so they now staked out on the Judean borders. This was an army that didn't know when it was defeated. They were driven back, but they still kept coming. This is important because we need to know that our challenger is rarely alone, but is usually part of a larger, wider, committed fighting unit. So don't expect your challenger to run away, or curl up and die. And even if they do, don't think that that is the end of the challenge. We can never say the battle is over. Look what happened to President George Bush when he prematurely announced in Iraq, "mission accomplished", because he misguidedly thought his only problem was Saddam Hussain. Goliath was no loner; he was a soldier in an army of trained soldiers with equipment to kill. How often because we failed to assess the challenge, we declared prematurely "mission accomplished", forgetting that after we have beaten off one soldier we still have the army from which they came to contend with! So remember, when your Goliath emerges he emerges from an army; he is not alone; he is part of a pack; in fact he is often their champion with others waiting in the wings competing to take his place.

Goliath cut a fearsome figure. He was huge. Standing six cubits and a span (1 Samuel 17.4), i.e. three metres, or over nine feet tall. We get a sense what this means if we skip a few chapters back to 1 Samuel 10.23-24 when Saul had been made king. There we are told that the prophet Samuel summoned all the people of Israel to Mizpah and when Saul stood up, he was a head taller that any of the others. Samuel at that time said to those gathered, "Do you see the man the Lord has chosen? There is no one like him among all the people". Tall as Saul was, he did not measure up to Goliath and was in fact as afraid of him as were the other shorter men. David's challenger was fearfully tall. But Goliath was not just a big trained soldier, the man from Gath was also a champion fighter. He was most probably used to fighting in one to one combat. Saul told David that whereas he was a mere boy, Goliath had been a fighting man from his youth (1 Samuel 17.33). And we must be in no doubt about the psyche of Goliath: he had a lot resting upon that huge frame and armour. If he lost, the Philistine army and people lost, with servitude to their avowed enemy as the consequence. But, really, when one looked at Goliath and looked at David, it was the battle of little and large; the chances of Goliath losing would have seemed farfetched, to say the least.

This huge imposing man was equipped to the teeth with the very latest and best armoury, as befitted a champion soldier. Standing at over nine feet, he also had on a bronze helmet, a bronze body armour weighing 125 pounds or 57 kilograms (or almost 9 stones, probably as heavy as David!), and bronze greaves protected his legs. To complete his armour, slung over Goliath's back was a javelin that commentators say is best described as a sword with a curved blade like a sickle; then a spear with an iron point and a shaft like a weaver's beam and used like a sling; the point of Goliath's spear weighed over a stone at 15 pounds, 7 kilograms. To complete his protection, Goliath had a shield, probably a large rectangular one, affording maximum protection. And his army provided him with an armour-bearer (I smile when I think of what the term 'armour bearer' has come to mean in parts of today's church). No wonder Goliath was confident! Wouldn't you be if you were three metres tall with all this protective and offensive gear, and with an armour-bearer to boot?

And so from this lofty position, bigger than anyone else, well trained, well armed, well supported, Goliath looked at David and scorned him. He despised him. Understanding your challenge means being in no doubt about how the enemy sees you, his intentions toward you. As Satan said to God about Job, do you think he serves you for nought? You move that fence you have around him and his family and see if he does not curse you to your face. He serves you because you prosper everything his hands touch, and because his herds and flocks flourish. Take these from him and I promise you he will desert you (Job 1.9-11). You need to know that the devil believes your faith is a cynical and self-serving one that folds when the going gets tough. In hard times, the devil expects you to desert camp, jump ship. When the blessing dries up we are expected to dry up too, and sadly we sometimes do. The enemy despises you and your faith and has only one desire towards you, to sift you as wheat (Luke 22.31). As David advanced towards him, Goliath, resplendent in his great size and attack proof armour, armour-bearer in tow, took a good look at his opponent, David, and saw only a boy: ruddy and handsome, but a boy none the less (1 Samuel 17.42). One reason why he could get such a good look at him is because David had no helmet on – in fact the boy had on normal clothes. But looks are deceiving. Scripture says, "The weapons we fight with are not the weapons of the world. They have divine power to demolish strongholds. We demolish arguments and every pretension that sets itself up against the knowledge of God, and we take captive every thought to make it obedient to Christ" (2 Corinthians 10.4-5). The understanding Christian is not frightened or undermined by the enemy's scorn.

Seeing David, Goliath's reading of the situation probably was that if after 40 days of challenging Israel to send him a man of their choice to come and fight for the honour, dignity, and freedom of Israel in a winner takes all man to man combat, if David was the best Israel could offer, Israel was in bad shape. He misread the situation! Goliath shouted to David, "Am I a dog that you come to me with sticks?" If he were Jamaican he would have asked him, "is weh yu tink yu a go wid sling shat?" "Boy", he said, "come here let me give your young flesh to the birds of the air and the beasts of the field!" (1 Samuel 17.44). He was under-whelmed with his opponent, and what a contrast they must have cut on that battlefield: a strong man versus a weakling. Seen through human eyes, a no contest. But God keeps reminding us, "my grace is sufficient for you, for my power is made perfect in weakness" (1 Corinthians 12.9). How true, as God told Samuel earlier, that "man looks at the outward appearance, but the Lord looks at the heart" (1 Samuel 16.7).

Friends, if we are to successfully handle our greatest challenges, understanding their nature, their character is crucial. Things are never as they appear. The gift of discernment is one the Holy Spirit gives.

THE SIGNIFICANCE OR IMPLICATIONS OF THE CHALLENGES WE FACE

How we perceive the challenges we face, in terms of their source and purpose, largely determines our attitude to them. If we perceive challenges, or what the counselling fraternity calls, 'problem situations and unused opportunities'[1] as coming from demonic sources and therefore harmful in intent, then we face them with foreboding, if we face them at all. But the Bible instructs us to "consider it pure joy, whenever you face trials of many kinds, because you know that the testing of your faith develops perseverance. Perseverance must finish its work so that you may be mature and complete, not lacking anything" (James 1.2-3 NIV). It is therefore important that we face challenges positively, viewing them as the manure that succours and the vitamins that strengthen us.

In 'The Martyrdom of Polycarp'[2] the story is told of the 2nd century Bishop of Smyrna, Polycarp. The manner in which he faced his greatest challenge has gone down in history as a model for all believers. He chose martyrdom when faced with renouncing his faith in the Lord Jesus or die. To get off, all he had to say was, "Caesar is Lord". But Polycarp chose and embraced death, "that he might fulfil his appointed destiny of being made a sharer with Christ". It is recorded that when he was arrested, he immediately ordered that a table be set for his captors to eat and drink as much as they wished. Then he prayed for two hours in their presence, having asked for one hour. Then when brought before the proconsul in the stadium that was to be the place of his death, his accusers having found him to be a gentle and gracious man in his eighties, became sympathetic towards him and begged him to give them a reason not to throw him to the wild beasts or in the fire. "Just swear by the genius of Caesar", they pleaded. "Swear the oath and I will release you, revile Christ", the proconsul said. Polycarp responded, "for eighty-six years I have been his servant, and he has done me no wrong. How can I blaspheme my King who saved me?" (p139). And choosing death by fire, he was burned alive; though they had to stab him to kill him because legend says the fire refused to consume his body. How we face our greatest challenges depend on how we perceive their source and purpose.

A great truth that is often difficult to grasp, but which helps us as we face great challenges, is that often it's not really about you at all. In 'The Martyrdom of Polycarp' we find this, "it is the mark of true and steadfast love to desire not only that oneself be saved, but all the brothers as well" (p135). In other words, in our hour of greatest challenge, our greatest ally is not self-love, self-preservation or self-interest, but the love, preservation and interest of others. Your greatest challenge is invariably, and needs to be, bigger than you. It must serve a greater purpose. The challenge David faced in Goliath was really not about David. Not about David's personal salvation or survival. Many of us fail because we mistakenly think it's all about 'me'. In fact I want to suggest that 'meism' is now a pseudo-god that fails to deliver at our greatest moment of challenge. This false-god is staking its claim for me-worship.

Biblical scholar John Drane suggests that we are in the midst of a paradigm shift of massive proportions towards a post-modern phenomenon called 'New Age'. Drane calls it a vast and amorphous collection of practices and beliefs of a vaguely 'spiritual' kind.[3] Professor Walter Brueggemann describes this post-modern climate as one that recognises that there is no given definition (of anything) and that rival claims must simply be argued out.[4] I believe we see this for example in the popular form of 'me worship' that has been challenging for space instead of true worship of God. We continue to sing "it's all about you", but really it's all about me: my blessing, or as one preacher put it recently 'my stuff'. The David versus Goliath example challenges this 'me' spirit that is now sweeping the Christian church, wreaking havoc as it goes like a hurricane. We need a greater cause when we face our challenges than ourselves; greater reasons to fast, pray and travail than personal blessings. We should never forget Jesus' words in the Gospels, "do not worry, saying, what shall we eat, or what shall we drink? Or what shall we wear? For the pagans run after all these things and your heavenly father knows that you need them. But seek first his kingdom and his righteousness and all these things will be given to you as well" (Matthew 6.31-33). When we are consumed by ourselves, when we go to church to get our blessings, we inevitably ignore the corporate body, community and world needs, including our responsibility to the poor and needy. Again I say our greatest challenges represent that which is bigger than ourselves.

Let's look at how David's challenge had implications way beyond himself. David recognised these wider implications from the time he drew near to the scene of the battle. He overheard the soldiers speaking about how Goliath kept defying Israel (1 Samuel 17.25), not just King Saul or the soldiers gathered to fight. Every time Goliath stepped out and belched his challenge without a response, the whole nation of Israel was being defied. David described it as defying the armies of the living God and as a 'disgrace' (v26) that needed to be removed from Israel. As David experienced the environment of panic and fear amongst Israel's soldiers, an indignant spirit rose up in him and he thought, in the words of one commentator, "no one, no matter how powerful, how tall, how heavily armoured, no one should presume to insult God and the people of God in this way" (p126).[5] To further paraphrase David, 'this uncircumcised Philistine has shamed Israel before the birds of the air, the beasts of the field, the soldiers on the battlefield and the world outside' (1 Samuel 17.46-47). And in the face of such public shame, a public witness to God's power was needed. As a result, people of faith would be encouraged and strengthened, unbelievers confounded. Our world today, like David's then, has many doubting, frightened believing soldiers unable to face up to their Goliaths, and the David spirit today like David's spirit then has a great responsibility to take on the giant; to encourage and restore the fainthearted that it can be known again that there is a God in Israel, mighty to save. So remember, when your test comes its outcome does not affect you alone. Whether you succeed or fail will have wider ramifications, and this knowledge, this awareness, must inform our behaviour.

THE PREPARATION NEEDED FOR THE CHALLENGES WE FACE

Here are two competing points of view that help me to highlight the need for preparation for the challenges we face. On the one hand, 'what you see is what you get'. On the other hand, 'don't judge a book by its cover'. Both have their merit. In the case of David, Goliath would have done well not to judge a book by its cover. David's appearance was deceptive indeed. Today, we do well to remember not to take anyone at face value, including those who say, 'what you see is what you get'; because you never know what's hidden from view. You see, David looked for all the world like an inquisitive, mischievous young man, suited only for running errands for his brothers who were the men of war. But that was only until it became clear where he'd been, what he'd been up to and what God had done to and with him. Goliath or anyone else, including David's brothers, could not tell by looking, what preparation David had undergone. Be careful how you treat people, even the most innocuous and feeble looking amongst us. It may not be obvious that you are in the presence of greatness. Hebrews 13.2 says some have entertained angels without knowing it.

To handle your greatest challenges well, you need to undergo preparation. The old song says, "Have thine own way Lord, have thine own way; Thou art the potter I am the clay, mould me and make me after thy will, whilst I am waiting yielded and still." Preparation! Preparation! Preparation! I am reminded of this little refrain I heard Bishop Jeff Atherley with at Tolmers Camp Site many years ago, and which I repeated in a sermon on BBC Radio 4 Sunday Service last year on Pentecost Sunday. "To walk with God no strength is lost, walk on; to talk with God no breath is lost, talk on; to wait on God no time is lost, wait on". Friends, we are going to have to learn to wait in the preparation bay long enough to have our character moulded and made by God and God's manufacturing agents. Some people think you are lucky; they think it's because you've sold your soul; they call you an overnight success when God elevates you. They weren't there when you took risks, when you went without, when you fasted and prayed and studied night and day. They only see you when you've come over. They didn't see you when you were going through the valley of the shadow of death, when God himself had to hold you tight and tell you to open and read the 23rd Psalm, and remind you to 'fear not'. So when they look at you, they don't see that history. Truth is, just like Goliath did not know what or who he was looking at, so too many will look at you, but they really don't know you. They can't see that steel rod in your backbone, put there during the divine moulding process, so when they try to bend and twist you, they can't. How can they know, they weren't there when you were being painfully taken apart, re-moulded and re-made. And now, you may be not much to look at, but you're deep, you're strong, you're indestructible. You endured your years of study and preparation.

What Goliath couldn't have known about David is that at a secret anointing ceremony that took place some time previously, God had instructed Samuel the prophet/priest to anoint David king of Israel. At the time of the anointing, the boy was in the field tending the sheep and even Samuel expected God's choice to be one of the elder brothers. But when they finally called him from the field, God told Samuel, this is the one, rise and anoint him king (1 Samuel 16.12). And from that day, Scripture says, the Spirit of the Lord came upon David in power (v13). But not much changed! David went back to tending the sheep. Except that, as he would tell Saul at the moment of his great encounter with Goliath, whilst tending the sheep in the desert whenever a lion or a bear came and carried off a sheep from the flock, he went after it, struck it and rescued the sheep. When the killer beast that could knock out its victim with a paw turned on this boy, he being full of the Spirit of the Lord would catch it by its hair, strike it and kill it (1 Samuel 17.34-35). 'So, King Saul, I may not look like much, but I have been prepared for this moment and the means by which I overcame those wild beasts, will deliver me from this Philistine' David might have said.

David's character, his strong faith in divine power didn't just descend upon him in that moment on the battlefield; it had been shaped in the desert, in the inglorious job of keeping his father's sheep. Can you imagine the adrenalin rush when you overcome a lion or a bear? There, he discovered a braveness and a fearlessness he never knew he had. He learned to trust the power of the Spirit because he knew in his own strength he could never overpower a lion or a bear. He learned that his superhuman response was not for his own deliverance, but in defence of the defenceless lambs of his father. The power of God in him was not for his own protection, but in protection of the sheep under his care. Goliath would not have known that this innocent, armourless, helmetless young man, 'a boy' as he called him, had already slain a lion and a bear. You can't judge a book by its cover. It is so easy to underestimate people, not knowing that their roots are beneath the surface of where you can see.

In facing up to our greatest challenge we need to be tough and tender. David was not just a deceptive looking tough man, he had a tender side too. He learned to be moved with compassion into action in defence of his father's sheep, and was equally moved when he observed the plight of God's people faced with being ridiculed by the Philistine giant. When God says David was a man after his own heart, we are reminded that Hebrews 4 tells us that we do not have a high priest who is unable to sympathise with our weakness (v15). Allow me to interject that some people in David's position that day would have been so busy criticising his brothers, the king, the army, not to mention the civil servants and generals – that they would have failed to engage Goliath. David didn't do that; he leapt to the defence of Israel and God's good name. He was a mere visitor to the battlefield but could not stand aside and watch the humiliation of his people. We need to learn to cultivate our sensitive side.

Often we have no idea what God through life is preparing us for. But then when we have been prepared, it's amazing how often we stumble upon our destiny. David was merely running an errand, and whilst there he overheard the plight of Israel and the reward King Saul had offered. David remembers his experience with the lion and the bear and for a moment thought that God must have brought him to the battlefield for such a time as that. What for you may be an accident or coincidence is something God had been planning, training you for behind the scenes. Then suddenly, seemingly by happenchance, the God-appointed time comes. And the Spirit in you rises up; cometh the hour, cometh the man!

Part of David's experience was coping with jealousy and do-gooders. It was not the other soldiers, but David's elder brother who taunted him. In anger probably borne of jealousy, he said, "you conceited and wicked little boy, why have you come here, and what have you done with our father's few sheep?" (1 Samuel 17.28). David brushed him off with, what have I done wrong now?

But if you think jealous people are your greatest challenge, try those who just want to be helpful but don't know the score. Once David persuaded Saul to let him go and fight Goliath, the same Saul who with his men had been too coward to fight against Goliath now wants to be David's special adviser on armoury. Bless him. Saul meant well but was not there when Samuel anointed David, or when David killed the lion and bear. So now he's just trying to help. This reminds us to beware those who are well meaning but ill-informed as to your challenge. The king who would not put on this armour and go fight Goliath, is keen to put his armour on David (v38): his coat of armour, bronze helmet, his sword over his tunic; all this he put on David.

David was in Saul's clothes ready to go and meet his greatest challenge. But you can't wear another man's clothes to fight your battle. Saul's armour and staff just did not fit David. Let me say to the young men and women here today, you may be young, but the God who has been putting you through your training also want you to train up your mind to be independent enough to hear and obey him. Don't become so institutionalised that whatever the king says you say yes. David did Saul the courtesy of trying them on, but then said, "I cannot go in these, I'm not used to them" (v39). And so he took them off, and picked up what was his armoury: his shepherd's bag, his staff, five smooth stones from the stream and a sling. And off he went into combat with the supremely armoured Goliath. Some folks want you to wear their armoury so they can take or share in the glory. But the glory belongs to God. As you face your greatest challenge wear your own clothes, use your own words and your own style; face it in the might of the Spirit God has put into you. Don't mimic anybody.

THE COURAGE TO ACTUALISE VICTORY OVER THE CHALLENGES WE FACE

It is not enough to understand intellectually the nature of the challenge, its significance and the preparation needed. After all is said and done victory has to be grasped. Some wise person says, power is never given, it is only ever taken. So, as soon as David was close enough to Goliath to tell him, he told him, "you come against me with sword and spear and javelin, but I come against you in the name of the Lord Almighty, the God of the armies of Israel, whom you have defied" (1 Samual 17.45). Two matters are worth noting right here in these final rites. David said, "the Lord will deliver you into my hand and I will strike you and take your head off" (v46). Try to look past the gruesomeness of beheading referred to here. The key message is that in our challenge God works and we work.

God will deliver Goliath into your hands but you have to strike him and cut off his head. The symbolisms are great here. I wonder how many of us have experienced God delivering our Goliath into our hands, but have been unwilling to finish the job off. That thing in your life that taunted you, mocked you, threatened you, that you were in fear of for forty days, and now God has delivered it into your hands; he has worked things out for you, and still you cannot bring yourself to kill it and cut off its head. Administer the final rites. As the heavily armed giant Goliath approached, the boy reached for a stone, put it in his sling and by the help of God found the one chink in Goliath's armour. Great was the fall. David pounced to finish the job and the Philistines fled in defeat.

Things don't always work out as planned or expected. Upon David's triumph over Goliath, the Philistines ran off and did not fulfil their promise that they would become Israel's servants. Don't expect the enemy to keep his promise. His word is not his bond. Neither was Saul quick to fulfil his promise to exempt David and his family from taxes, or to let David marry his daughter. Every gain had to be fought for. And to show how success does not always bring peace and harmony, Saul became jealous of David and till his death tried to kill him. But, the act of defeating Goliath was done.

Why is it important that we complete the victory God has handed to us? So that the enemy's camp knows that God is real. That the birds, beasts, soldiers and the world which knew that Goliath was an imminent threat, know that by the power of God he is now dead. So that people will know that God does not save by the might of the sword or spear. Might is not right. It's important that we complete our greatest challenge so the world knows that there is a God in Israel and that the battle is his (1 Samuel 17.47). As one commentator points out, this was no ordinary battle, but one in which God's honour was at stake, and in this circumstance Israel and David's exposure to danger permitted God's honour to be more acknowledged than if David had more obviously been a match for the Philistine.[6]

IDENTIFYING THE GREATEST CHALLENGE WE FACE TODAY

The manner in which David faced up to Goliath is a great example to us today about how we should face out greatest challenges, in all their complexities: including divine intervention, desert experiences of victory over adversities, family jealousies, personal egos, well-meaning help that has to be discarded, and much more. But a key lesson we might learn from the David/Goliath encounter is the need to be a big person in more than physical size. Goliath was big in physical stature, but David was big spiritually, emotionally and aspirationally. Big problems, big challenges require big people. How big are you? Apostle Paul posed this as a challenge when addressing the Corinthian church, "Brothers, I could not address you as spiritual but as worldly – mere infants in Christ. I gave you milk, not solid food, for you were not yet ready for it. Indeed you are still not ready. You are still worldly, for since there is jealousy and quarrelling among you, are you not worldly?" (1 Corinthians 3.1-3). Little things please little minds, it is said.

I suggest to you today that our biggest challenge at present is that too many of us are too small! And all of us must take responsibility for that. Am I my brother's keeper? Yes! If my brother is still in short pants, sucking his thumb, drinking milk, still has his milk teeth, growth stunted; it's not just his fault – it's mine too. Neither is the fault only personal, it's organisational and institutional. Some institutions have developed into bodies that deny or at best do not encourage human, spiritual and intellectual flourishing. Might we have developed the art of keeping people small? Inadvertently, may be. I am thinking of the many young men and women I grew up with in this church and how many of us have managed to stand tall in the church let alone the world. Only a few. Many languish in mediocrity, not because of a lack of potential but because of a lack of appropriate nurture, investment, development and the space to innovate and grow. Any system that is heavily judgemental and legalistic stunts the growth that grace would allow. If you grow up in a home where parents 'kunk' you in your head when you make mistakes, then don't be surprised if your educational, physical and other development is stunted. Too many of our people of great potential have been lost. We must grow, not just the few, but the masses, into big people.

A key model for growing big people is found in Ephesians 4.11-16, which we may have turned on its head by prioritising perfection ahead of equipping the saints for the work of ministry. Our first task, on a personal and corporate level, is to equip the saints – with their faults and failures. All of the ministries in the churches have been given to equip the saints for ministry; to put people to work – not just within the four walls of the church – so that everyone can become big people with jobs, vocations, feeling fulfilled, valued and of worth before God and man. It is through the preparation and practice of God's people for service that the body is built up, and reaches unity in faith and knowledge and becomes mature, attaining the whole measure of the fullness of Christ. When did you last sit down with someone, a new or an old convert, and in prayer discuss what ministry they have from God and how on a daily, weekly, monthly, yearly basis you can as pastor, teacher, apostle, prophet, evangelist help equip that person for service in the church and wider world? Or are we preoccupied with sitting in Moses' seat of judgement rather than Jesus' seat of grace, pardon, forgiveness, generosity and boundless, conditionless love?

Recently I paid a visit to the headquarters of the Elim Church, in my work with Churches Together in England. There we met officials of the Elim Church in England. John Glass the national Superintendent gave me a copy of his new book, 'Building Bigger People'.[7] In his book, John shares that a key objective of ministry is to build individuals who reflect what is meant by the well-rounded Hebrew word 'Shalom' with its sense of wholeness that permeates the body, soul and spirit. He goes on to say, "Bigger people, who live with a sense of wholeness, are capable of handling bigger challenges that lead to greater opportunities of ministry and service" (p2). John observes that God rarely if ever entrusts big responsibility to small minds and timid hearts. If this is true, and I believe it to be, then it means that any local, national or international church or even secular organisation that does not build big people will not have the human resource to build big congregations or businesses. When big challenges come, big men and women meet those challenges; the weak and timid fail to meet them and even if they are not killed, they do not prosper.

The challenge before us today is simple: individually, corporately we must be big enough to face our greatest challenges. On a personal level, you need to take responsibility for your growth. You must discover and actualise your potential, your destiny in life. Like David, God will have been presenting you with opportunities to slay lions and bears in the backwater, out of the glare of the limelight. What you do in those times is crucial for when you meet your Goliath on the battlefield. God is cultivating in you the qualities you need, and in the meantime you may be overlooked for a while; someone may be in the place God has anointed you to be and you have to wait. You may even have to play the harp to calm them in their times of madness; you may have to serve the one you will one day govern. But like David you must learn that what God has anointed you to do, you will do in God's time.

My pastor, T A McCalla, used to say to us as young men growing up, "build up yourself". I now know what he meant. You have to build up yourself in your most holy faith. And let me be frank, if the environment you are in, if the ministry that feeds you is making you shrink, you must take responsibility for yourself – either leave and find new pastures that feed you and build you up, or get in there and shake things up. But, do not stay in an environment that is underwhelming and which, even after years of so-called nurturing, leaves you a spiritual skeleton without healthy flesh, strong bones and muscles that should make you a big person. And by the way, the reason it's important that you become a big person is not for selfish gain, it is so that you can bring about the defeat of the Goliaths that exalt themselves against God's people and God's name.

CONCLUSION

So, in conclusion, the David/Goliath challenge teaches us that we need to grow into big people, equal to the tasks that face us in our time. Whether the challenge is spiritual, social, economic, political, cultural, or even racial, the David/Goliath encounter teaches us that we need to be big people to defeat what looks like overwhelming odds. But to get there I have argued that we need to understand the nature or character of the challenges we face; understand the significance or implications of the challenges we face; prepare to meet the challenges we face; have the courage actualise victory over the challenges we face; and identify that the greatest challenge we face today is to be big men and women. Are you big enough to face your big challenge?

Sermon preached in Regional Convention of Church of God of Prophecy, London 2010

1. Gerard Egan, The Skilled Helper 6th Edition 1998
2. J B Lightfoot (ed) The Apostolic Fathers 1989
3. John Drane, Cultural Change and Biblical Faith, 2000
4. Walter Brueggemann, The Bible and Post-modern Imagination 1993
5. Joyce Baldwin (ed), Tyndale Old Testament Commentaries, 1 & 2 Samuel
6. Joyce Baldwin (ed) p 128
7. John Glass, Building bigger people, 2008

CHAPTER 14

Black theology – continuity and change

INTRODUCTION

In attempting to address the theme of this auspicious occasion, I want to make a case for the British Black theology enterprise, or project, which is still in its embryonic stage and therefore needs all of our nurture and support. I do so because I believe that this fledgling discipline is the real outcome of what we have come to know as the Centre for Black and White Christian Partnership. I believe that in time, British Black theology will be seen as its enduring legacy. Let me then seek to justify this position by examining what British Black theology is, who it is for and what is its probable destiny.

WHAT IS BRITISH BLACK THEOLOGY?

BRITISH

What does it mean to be British these days? In her book, 'Who Do We Think We Are: Imaging The New Britain', Yasmin Alibhai-Brown recounts an interview on the Today programme on BBC Radio 4 in September 2000. The interviewer was James Naughtie and the interviewees were herself and Lord Tebbit - he of the 'cricket test'. I remember listening to the encounter – I don't know if anyone else here recalls it.

The catalyst was an anonymous population forecaster who predicted that on current trends, White Anglo-Saxons would become a minority in Britain at some unspecified time in the future. The liberal thinker Alibhai-Brown, who is of Asian, African and British heritage and married to an Anglo-Saxon, argued that the discussion was predicated upon an absurdity, since, as she put it, "we are all British now, people of this place". She further criticised the demographer and others who she says seem to live in a constant state of heightened anxiety about such matters. Lord Tebbit responded: "I regret very much that as soon as anybody enters into this arena of debate, and it is important for public policy that we do so, then they are abused by people like Ms or Mrs Brown or whoever she is …" Alibhai-Brown responded, "I have a name Lord Tebbit, my name is Yasmin Alibhai-Brown." "All right Miss or Mrs Ailbhai-Brown," said Lord Tebbit, "let's come to the point of multiracial and multicultural communities. Everywhere in the world where we see multicultural communities, we also see much social unrest. I would be happier if these were solved outside this country." Alibhai-Brown reminded Lord Tebbit of football hooligans and other maladjusted White Britons, who, she argued, did what they did without any help from multiculturalism. Lord Tebbit believed this comment was offensive to decent British people listening. Alibhai-Brown responded, "I too am British". There was a pause, during which James Naughtie prompted a response from Lord Tebbit, who then remarked, "Well, I am sure Ms Alibhai-Brown carries a British passport. I don't know whether she was born here."

These exchanges demonstrate something of the tension involved in defining Britishness. There are people on every side of this argument defining what it means to be British to suit their political and sociological thinking. And it is not as simple as saying that White people don't want Black people to become British. There are many Black people who are uncomfortable about being called English, Welsh, Irish, Scottish or indeed British. They wish to retain their original identity. Then there are those Whites for whom Whiteness and Britishness are synonyms. In their thinking, a passport counts for nothing, being born here counts for nothing, fighting and laying down your life for this country's wars count for nothing in terms of national identity. In this racial reasoning, a prerequisite to be British is to be White.

However, we do know some facts. For example, we know that Britain is a multi-ethnic society in which, according to the 1991 census, there were 54.9 million people, rising in the 2001 census to 58.8 million. In the 1991 census, 94.5% of the British population were White people of Anglo-Saxon, Irish, Greek, Turkish and other Europeans; 5.5% of the population were from minority ethnic groups such as Black of African, Caribbean and other descent, South Asian, Indian, Pakistani, Bangladeshi, Chinese and others. By 1991, the majority of the 5.5% were born in Britain. Preliminary results suggest that the 2001 census will show an increase in people from minority ethnic groups to 7.9%, still a long way off being the feared majority of alarmist demographers! And, of course, even more of this 7.9% will have been born in Britain.

By any definition of Britishness, whether based upon birth, heritage or passport, no one in Britain can with integrity claim that only the Whites in these statistics are British. What Britain has is a large White ethnic majority and a growing, but still small and diverse, minority ethnic population. What is needed is a new and shared understanding of what it means to belong to a Britain that is owned equally by all its citizens. As Bhikhu Parekh points out in his book, 'Rethinking Multiculturalism: Cultural Diversity and Political Theory', "belonging to a cultural community admits of much variation and is not homogeneous in nature" (p148). Britain is not, and truly never has been, a homogeneous, monoculture, mono-ethnic country. So my definition begins with staking a claim for ownership of what it means to be British for minority ethnic people who have either taken up citizenship or were born here. This is why I prefer terms like Black-British, Caribbean-British, African-British, Asian-British, et al., instead of African-Caribbean, for example. British Black Theology, I argue, begins with this issue of British belonging. One in which people of diverse heritages are unafraid to embrace that identity, having due regard to the past and to the present.

BLACK

What does it mean to be Black? The answer to this question depends upon whether one is a political pragmatist or an ethnic or racial essentialist. If you are a political pragmatist, then in the words of Robert Beckford, "Black is a complex ethnic-political description. On the one hand, it is a synonym for dark-skinned people - Africans, African Caribbean and Asians. On the other hand, it can encompass those who are not White, or those engaging in resistance to domination, or what I call, counter hegemonic resistance" (Dread and Pentecostalism, p 2). With this broad definition of Black, you could even be White and yet be Black, if you join the anti-oppression revolution. I believe there are some real difficulties as well as some benefits here. For example, human beings, in Britain and elsewhere, come in a long line of shades, a colour continuum we could say. This political alliance as a rallying point, or a flag of convenience, can bring together an otherwise disparate group of minorities in a solidarity that would be otherwise missing to challenge White supremacy and the racism that emanates from it. However, by isolating a few as White and grouping all the other shades together as Black, we run the risk of confirming an elitism upon this group, which is precisely what is being fought against. In my view therefore, Black as non-White has to be seen as a pragmatic and therefore short-term strategy.

If you are a Black essentialist, then Black is synonymous with Pan African identity and must be applied exclusively to people of African descent. Here, Ronald Nathan is very clear. In an article in the Journal of Black Theology he asks rhetorically, "when did Africans cease to be Black and when did Black cease to be African?" In this definition, political pragmatism is replaced by a geo-ethnic, or geo-racial specificity. This rather exclusive concept of Black requires a reordering of political colour-coding as applied in Britain. It argues that nobody else can be called Black apart from those of African heritage. This does of course simplify matters somewhat, but it is precisely this simplicity that runs this theory into difficulties. It seems fallacious to suggest that people of dark hue from non-African parts of the world should be denied their claim to Blackness, should they so wish to embrace it. Also, such is the mongrelisation of race around the globe that Black essentialism is as false a notion as White essentialism.

Some fall in neither camp; indeed, many dislike the term Black and wish it away. In a recent conversation a minister asked me, "why do we have to talk of 'Black'? It is so negative." I am quite convinced that the popular usage of the term Black in almost exclusively negative terms has meant that that most people, Black and White, view it negatively. From Black Wednesday, to black holes in the economy, to black days, to being blackballed, to being a blackleg, the list goes on. The usage of the term 'black' in popular speak is linked to its usage in medieval times when black equalled evil and white equalled good. We see this perpetuated in our times, as the popular caricature of angelic beings, including God, Jesus and the angels, is White. The devil is of course Black. In Sade's latest album, 'By Your Side', she tells the story of a child who did not appreciate the significance of his Black skin. A line says, "Didn't know what it meant to be Black, till they gave him his change and didn't want to touch his hand". So, there are those who would like to distance themselves from the term and what it means in contemporary society.

The truth is that there is no consensus about who or what is meant in Britain by Black. As Emmanuel Lartey points out, "paradoxically, it is people who others would call Black who most vociferously object to the usage of the term". Lartey continues to define Black as "people of African, Caribbean and Asian descent as well as people who identify with the Black experience in terms of heritage, oppression and domination" (JBTB, issue 3, 1999). At another level, the term Black stands in judgement against White supremacist thought and Black acquiescence to subservience. This judgement calls out, how dare people of whatever skin shade believe themselves better or less than another of God's handmade? It is here as we begin to reflect upon where God might stand in all of this that theology comes into the frame.

THEOLOGY

Theology as Emmanuel Lartey reminds us, is "God talk". Of course, talk is more than words, so theology is that which we think, do and say about God. Theology asks questions and seeks answers about human life and God's involvement with it. If we then reflect upon British Black Theology, we are asking questions about God in the life experiences of British Black people. It is here, too, that I get into squabbles with my Black, and sometimes White, colleagues. For, I refuse to be bound by a Black identity the only point of reference of which is opposition to White. My ethnic identity must stand in awe of God alone, who made me. Therefore, my Black identity is acceptable to me only if it relates to the whole of me who sometimes am son, brother, uncle, cousin, husband, father, scholar, ecumenist, chairman et al. I refuse to see myself as having an existence which is exclusively, or even primarily, in relation to White people. White and Black stand shoulder to shoulder with each other and before God. British Black Theology cannot therefore only be about the oppression/liberation dialectic. Such would be a narrow, demeaning and ungodly existence.

Part of a presentation on the closure of the Centre for Black and White Christian Partnership, Birmingham 2002

Part 5

ECUMENISM

CHAPTER 15

One but how?

INTRODUCTION

It was as long ago as December 2001 when I first heard of this ecumenical event. I understood its remit then as wanting to grapple with the issue of how we who are privileged to be Christians living at the start of the 21st century might seek to fulfil Jesus' prayer for the unity of his followers. My understanding of Christian unity is one predicated upon the quadrant concept of common worship, service, fellowship and witness. Much has been said about this in years gone by and we have added more words today, and so it is questionable whether what is needed are more words. I will try to be brief. Words seem particularly inadequate when we consider the events that have greeted us at the start of this new millennium. Events that appear to demand a Christian response.

It feels like crisis has followed crisis, culminating in recent times with events like the tragic shootings in my home town of Birmingham at the start of this year, which resulted in the deaths of two teenagers and the wounding of two others. This was by no means an isolated incident; it was not the first nor has it been the last, but it seems to have caught the public imagination. Some of us feel certain that these and other tragic events point to underlying social and political issues of declining moral and spiritual values in our society. These call for our urgent attention and Christian action. Words are not enough.

Then there has been that other recent crisis of the 'so-called' war on terror that led to the invasion of Iraq led by the United States and the United Kingdom. I only wish to note the mixed results of the ousting of President Saddam Hussein's regime: the cost of thousands of lives of civilians and military people, the maiming of thousands of others, the inability to discover any of the cocked and ready to use weapons of mass destruction, and the degree to which we appear to have stirred new waves of terror around the globe, adding to an already unstable situation. All this call for our attention and Christian action. Words are not enough.

Neither are words enough for the millions of minorities in Britain and the rest of Europe who feel discriminated against, and whose lives are made miserable by their exclusion from the benefits available in the mainstream of society, and the constant vulnerability of rootlessness and the loss of identity. Some of these are new arrivals as asylum seekers; others have been here for many years, but their colour and culture mark them out as different from the majority. Already since the new millennium, many have lost their lives while others continue to suffer racial attacks and abuse. If this were happening on the streets or at football matches only, it would be bad but not too bad. The truth is that the experience of many within the churches is little different. And this is not to deny the amount of effort going in to counter personal and institutionalised racism. These matters demand our attention and Christian action. Words are not enough.

But Christian action requires wisdom. An Old Testament text from 1 Chronicles points to the tremendous need we have today to have among us some people at least who can discern our times and know what we ought to do. Among those who went out to Ziklag to pledge their support for the emergent King David were mighty warriors bearing shields, commanders, leaders, young men, even some of David's own family members. The Chronicler notes too that among them were men of Issachar, who had understanding of the times, to know what Israel ought to do. One commentator suggests that this is a reference to their gifts of discernment of God's will for their day.[1] Others believe that these men were proficient in the disciplines of astronomical and physical science, and that the Chronicler was attempting to demonstrate that David had in his support those of the intelligent and learned classes, not just military men.[2] Whatever the apologetic may be, David appears to have had at his disposal some people who had discernment; men who understood the happenings of their day and how best to tackle them. Today, we need some people who, like the men of Issachar, understand our time and what we ought to do. Responding to our times will require today's church to have a united front in which our wisest minds and hearts speak up and all of us act up. I want to highlight three things that might help us answer the 'how' question together.

Probably the first job the 'Issacharians' among us have is to determine what we mean by unity, by being one. It strikes me that too many of us confuse being one with being the same. It is interesting, to me at least, that Jesus' passionate prayer in St John 17 makes no mention of ecclesial form, or doctrinal uniformity. His position, as the Head of the Church is very clear: "May they all be one as we are one". This is a oneness that allows me to retain my uniqueness, my particularity, yet not render me incompatible with you. It is a oneness that finds definition in Jesus himself, not in some manmade artificial determinant.

We can read this prayer either as a wish, or as a reality. I encourage you to read it as something realised. In Black Church tradition we have a saying which goes: "Jesus said it, I believe it, that makes it so". It is quite liberating when we embrace the understanding that we Christians, of whatever denomination, of whatever skin colour, of whatever nationality belong to the one catholic church of Jesus Christ. I don't know about your families, but I am one of eleven. We reside in three different countries, rarely meet, enjoy different levels of closeness, some of us don't really get on, but, but, but, we are the same mother and father's children. The basis of our intrinsic unity is our parentage. The position is quite simple, if you are my parents' child, you are my sibling. And so we can truly sing, "you're my brother you're my sister, so take me by the hand..."

The second job the 'Issacharians' among us have is to insist that we get to know one another. Our real problem is that though we are family, some of us have yet to meet each other on the level of understanding and empathy, share in each other's tradition, eat each other's food: spiritual and temporal. At the Centre for Black and White Christian Partnership which many of you have known and loved, we made a policy of Christians getting to know each other, brushing away the cobwebs of ignorance, paternalism and prejudice. As Black-led met White-led, Pentecostal met Quaker, Black Catholic met Black Anglican, so we were able to demythologise, learn and unlearn, and discover family we had hid from because we thought we were so different from them. It was here that I learned the meaning of respect and that it is not just esteem or regard, but from the Latin respecio: re – meaning 'back' and specio – meaning 'to look'. So, respect is to look back or again, implying to get to know, become familiar with, even to form relationship. Respect, I have resolved is about 'informed regard'. Christians deny ourselves vital resource, friendship, fellowship, nourishment, by not getting to know fellow brothers and sisters: children of our one heavenly father.

A third job the 'Issacharians' among us have is to find ways for us, the diverse family of God, to act together in worship, service, fellowship and witness. Whilst for the most part we live in our separate homes, as families do, we surely must develop and retain the ability to come together at times of family celebrations or tragedy. We have set up structures which many of us then ignore and rarely, if ever, use. We have already in place, the World Council of Churches, the British Council of Churches (now Churches Together in Britain and Ireland), national and local Churches Together instruments, Local Ecumenical Partnerships, Fraternals, Pulpit Swaps, other alliances like the Evangelical Alliance, Churches Councils, etc. Someone from Mars might ask us, what are all these for? It is a good question, because when the invasion of Iraq was in the making, we seemed, and still are, unable to come together to speak with one authoritative voice. When was the last time we laid aside our denominational straightjackets and celebrated together across colour, ethnicity, denominational and theological lines in honour of the one Lord Jesus who saved us? And when was the last time we truly washed each other's feet in sacrificial service?

There is an implicit inverse iniquity in that for as long as we remain unsure about our oneness, we may feel that we do not owe each other the Christian love our Lord has commanded of his children. However, by us accepting each other at face value as fellow Christians, embracing each other's hurts, anxieties, frustrations and ambitions, in solidarity confronting injustice and unrighteousness together, wherever it is found, will lead to the world believing that God is indeed in us in Christ reconciling all things unto himself. So, in the words of Fred Kaan, "Let us go out! Love people! In the here and now!" Amen.

Sermon at ecumenical symposium, St Albans 2006

1. Martin J Selman, Tyndale O T Commentaries
2. Jameson, Fauset, Brown, Bethany Parallel Commentary

CHAPTER 16

Unity with a purpose (based on Genesis 1.1-5; St John 17.20-23)

INTRODUCTION

As I get older, I make some silly mistakes. Like looking for my glasses whilst wearing them. You feel a little foolish when it dawns on you that they are actually on your face. If you're about my great age, you've probably done the same thing. The strange phenomenon of seeking what you already have is probably more common that we think: they say the grass is always greener on the other side. And, coming as I do from an early childhood in the Caribbean, I naturally have an inclination to recall sayings that remind me of important lessons. Like, 'cow never know the use of him tail till it cut off'. And since I'm in Scotland maybe we can talk about the Irish, can't we? You'll be familiar with the old joke of the traveller in Ireland who was lost and asked a local Irishman for directions, who said, "yes, I know where you need to go, but if I were you, I wouldn't start from here". Well brothers and sisters one of the most important piece of information for navigating on the roads as in life, is knowing who, where, what and why we are.

What I am talking about tonight may be described as 'realised ecumenism'. Could it be that the unity we seek we already have? Could it be that our failure to recognise where we are is hampering our abilities to fulfil our God-given purpose? Might we even be playing games with each other, wittingly or unwittingly, knowing that so long as I don't recognise you as my brother I don't have to treat you like a brother? Could it be that if we maintain the notion of a divided church we don't owe much love and respect to each other, but we will keep trying to become one church, and when we become that one church then we will love, respect and cooperate? Could it be that we are looking to structures where only relationships will do?

UNITY

Since the mid-1990s I have engaged in what I call 'intercultural ecumenism'. For me, this is an attempt to encourage unity between peoples and churches of not only different denominations, but of different ethnicities and cultures. I soon realised that my concept of greater mutual recognition and cooperation across cultures, ethnicities and denominations did not meet everybody's expectation of Christian unity. For some, nothing short of full visible union will do, and no efforts should be spared; indeed nothing worthwhile can be done, until we achieve it.

I guess we can all agree that schism, division, fragmentation is not reflective of a healthy body of Christ. Indeed, the Greek 'oikoumene' from which we get ecumenical implies more than cooperation, it implies wholeness. And what I think I have discovered since my initiation into the ecumenical world in the mid 1990s as Director of the Centre for Black and White Christian Partnership is that we are divided about what we mean by unity. As I've indicated, I lean towards growing cooperation leading to deeper togetherness, and I do so out of a conviction that the church of Jesus Christ is already one. I work on the basis that oneness is a given; it's in the DNA of the Church, and it is so not least because Jesus prayed for it: That all of them may be one as we are one (St John 17.21). Now, if we believe we don't have this unity and nothing can happen till we do, we may benefit from an examination of Jesus' words. Jesus' idea of unity is a compound one, "Father, make them one as we are one".

For those of us who embrace the understanding of God as Trinitarian, we bask in the incomprehensible notion that God is three and yet one, one yet three. We see here unity in diversity and diversity in unity. Whatever we may wish for, we do well not to take our diversity as an automatic signifier of disunity. I have ten siblings; we were given birth by one mother, and we have one father. Today we are all very different, live in different places; some of us don't even look alike. But we know we are of one stock and live with the challenge to demonstrate our shared heritage so that our parents' name is not dishonoured in the eyes of those who knew them. We are one, just not the same. Father, Son, Holy Spirit are one, just not the same. The church I beg to suggest is one, just not the same.

Here is a remarkable thing: God in Christ has already made one church, one called out people of different ethnicities, cultures and nations. John in a bit of realised eschatology saw us in Revelation 7.9, "After this I looked and there before me was a great multitude that no one could count, from every nation, tribe, people and language, standing before the throne and in front of the Lamb." Believe me, God has already done it, and we should affirm our oneness in Christ not as something to aspire to but as something done and sealed in the redemptive blood of Christ.

PURPOSE

Why has God made us one? I want to suggest tonight that we are one for a divine purpose. A purpose we run the risk of missing so long as we fail to embrace our oneness. In John 17 Jesus is clear, "Father make them one that the world may believe you have sent me". Even the oneness of the Godhead has a purpose. In Genesis we see the Father using the Word (Jesus the eternal Son) to speak creation into existence. Then we see the Holy Spirit moving to bring order out of chaos. Creation is the result of cooperation between the three in one.

Our challenge today is not to be one; our challenge is to live out practically what it means to be the one united brothers and sisters we are in Jesus Christ. Let me re-emphasise this thought; we have our oneness as an inheritance in the same way we inherit our physical siblings. Now let's live like brothers and sisters. The Psalmist says, "Behold how good and how pleasant it is when brothers/sisters dwell together in unity". The reverse is true; we could render this, "behold how bad and how unpleasant it is when brothers/sisters dwell together in disunity". It is more than semantics for me that we should cease trying to be one and accept that as a God-given reality, and focus our attention upon relationship, loving one another in the way brothers and sisters should, and cooperating with one another the way a people who worship the one God should, irrespective of what church we belong to. None of us is church by ourselves; we are only ever church together. One shall chase a thousand; two shall put ten thousand to flight. We are stronger together, weaker apart.

Brothers and sisters, here is what is at stake. Jesus came to this planet in the incarnation, the Word made flesh, fully God fully man.

He came to be the fulfilment of all things, and to show us what the invisible God really is like. He came with a plan of salvation that pointed a wayward humanity back to the Creator. But to get that message to the world, requires all of us to do it, because the gifts and talents and wisdom and energy are spread across the church, are everywhere present but are not present everywhere. When we exclude the other brother or sister because of colour, language, or nationality or tribe, we limit the image of Jesus being seen in what that other has to offer.

CONCLUSION

We will address issues around human trafficking much better when we have all the talents available involved. We who are called to be light and salt will be ever more effective when we recognise the other light and salt, not as competition but as an extension of what we are trying to do. So I have come to Glasgow tonight to say whether you are Black or White or somewhere between, we are one in Christ; now let us intentionally live as though we were. Our diversity is strength, not a weakness as we show Jesus to a diverse world that they may believe in the salvation he has brought. God has a purpose for our unity. It is that the world may believe. Amen.

Address given at an annual Churches Racial Justice Sunday ecumenical service in Glasgow 2010

CHAPTER 17

The ecumenical significance of Pentecostalism

INTRODUCTION

Ecumenism speaks of a diverse church's journey towards realising the unity for which Jesus prayed. It seeks to model itself on the unity of the Godhead of Father, Son and Holy Spirit. In the divine triune model, diversity is maintained and unity is attained; three in one and one in three. Pentecostalism can be described as one piece of an ecclesiological patchwork, or a peg of an ecclesiological orange. Its challenge is to be, and be accepted as, a legitimate part of the whole church reflecting unity in diversity, being one yet not all the same. We might begin by asking, what does Pentecostalism as a distinct component of the church bring to the body united?

Experts tell us that Pentecostalism is now the fastest-growing sector of the world church. Indeed, Pentecostals and Charismatics were estimated to constitute 27% of world Christianity in the mid-1990s and projected to become 44% by 2025. The growth is largely non-European, being African, Asian and Latin American. Britain, although clearly identifying with the decline in Christianity in Europe, is experiencing growth among Christians from African, Asian and Latin American backgrounds. Also, it is now the case that the Pentecostal and Charismatic experience touches all churches, and is therefore not the preserve of explicit 'Pentecostal Churches'. In my view this is right, and I want to use this talk to suggest that one of the ecumenical projects that could rejuvenate the church in these islands is the mainstreaming of the Pentecostal and Charismatic experience.

I do not believe God ever intended to establish Pentecostal Churches as somehow separate from the rest. Like other movements, Methodism and Evangelicals for example, the purveyors of Pentecostalism as a rejuvenating act of God – a kind of shot in the arm for the church –reacted to resistance to change by the main body by dogmatising their experience, resulting in further division in the Body of Christ. I believe that with a little imagination, humility and openness to each other Pentecostalism could have a far-reaching and reviving impact upon the Church of Jesus Christ, enabling it to engage more effectively in its Christ-centred mission of taking the gospel of liberation, life in abundance, to the people of this land.

I want to proceed by looking at some of the features of Pentecostalism and how they could impact the whole church for good in a key act of ecumenism, or cross-fertilisation. This is not a well-researched paper, just some initial thoughts for further study and research.

DIVINE IMMEDIACY

I begin with the Pentecostal belief in the immediate presence of God through the Holy Spirit. This is rooted in the understanding that Jesus in his parting promised to send another comforter, teacher to be with his followers; a presence that would empower them to do the work he assigned them. Pentecostals believe that Acts 2.1-4 is the fulfilment of that promise and that God through the Holy Spirit baptism now lives in, with and through us, and will so do "till the end of the age". I'm with Harvey Cox when he suggests that the fundamental contribution of Pentecostalism is "the reshaping of religion in the 21st century". Imagine what would happen to the church of Jesus Christ in the world were we to embrace the Pentecostal understanding that the Holy Spirit is not something 'out there' but someone powerful, right here. How would we behave were we to embrace the promise "and you shall receive power after that the Holy Spirit is come upon you"? According to the BBC website, "Pentecostalism is a form of Christianity that emphasises the work of the Holy Spirit and the direct experience of God by the believer". Why should not this be the perspective of every believer? When we read of the Holy Spirit filling the room where the early disciples waited for the promised coming, we sense this immediacy of the invisible God made visible in tongues of fire and made real in the supernatural experience of the disciples. And it is this experience that modern day Pentecostals like our antecedents John Wesley, Charles Finny, William Seymour and more claimed in order that the Christian life is lived in a transformative way. This happens when the spiritually dead has been made alive by the supernatural power of God through what we have come to know as the Holy Spirit.

Its not only Pentecostals that should embrace the immediacy of God, all Christians should: the Pope, the archbishop, the bishop, the minister, the laity; all of us should live in the immediate presence of God. And if this spirit orientation sometimes takes us into a trancelike state, like John on the isle of Patmos, so be it! What splendour we could experience! Pentecostals should consider it part of our duty to the body to share this understanding of the immediacy of God with our fellow brothers and sisters. My suspicion is that Pentecostals will find that this understanding is not the exclusive terrain of them alone. In fact I would go so far as to say, Christians may find that this sense of the immediate presence of the diving is not the preserve of followers of the Christian faith alone. Recently a Jewish colleague informed me that there is an expression of being filled with the Spirit in Judaism as well.

LOVE OF BIBLE

Pentecostals love the Bible, especially the King James Version (KJV). And while the majority do not possess the tools to do hermeneutics well, we cling to our heritage of a belief in verbal-plenary inspiration and inerrancy of Scripture. Evangelicals and Pentecostals vigorously embrace the concept of verbal-plenary inspiration of Scripture, something that Gordon Campbell in his helpful book to mark the 400th anniversary of the KJV says became a shibboleth for many conservative Evangelicals in the 19th century. It would be revealing, I think, to explore the reasons behind the 'Bible love' of especially Black Pentecostals, but suffice to say it exists and runs deep. The converse of this is a view of the Bible that is marked by scepticism about its reliability, and liberalism in interpretation. This is often marked by the saying, 'you mustn't take the Bible literally', or something like that. What I believe Pentecostals bring to the ecumenical table is a challenge to the general church as to the seriousness we all should accord our Holy Scripture, notwithstanding the background noise concerning translation flaws, etc. Because surely, since we believe in Jesus as the living Word of God, as the logos which existed with and as God in the beginning, we don't have to take a microscope to the

Bible, but instead regard the written Word as a static version of the living Word that is Jesus – we find our answers in the interaction between the two.

SPIRITUAL GIFTS

Pentecostals make an issue of the gifts of the spirit, and insist that all believers have been given gifts by God as it pleases him. It is a source of regret, for me, that classical Pentecostals tend to make a-priori speaking in tongues as the initial evidence of the Holy Spirit baptism of the believer. They have taken the experience of Acts 2.4 and transformed it into dogma. There is in my view absolutely no need to do so. Simply because we read that they all were filled with the Holy Spirit and spoke in tongues, cannot mean that from then on, irrespective of previous experiences of the Spirit and later experiences, that tongues must be essentialised over and above other spiritual gifts like prophecy, word of wisdom, faith, miracles, etc. But Pentecostalism has rejuvenated interest and awareness in the biblical understanding that Christians have been baptised into the Holy Spirit to give us power, energy and wisdom for ministry. These supernatural gifts are in and with us and we should expect to be exercised in and by them. We therefore need to take time to identify and grow into whatever gifts the Spirit has entrusted to each of us.

On the specific matter of the Pentecostal emphasis on tongues, with some regarding it as the 'initial evidence' of being baptised in the Holy Spirit, others viewing it as one of the gifts of the Spirit, it is worth recalling that at its first outing in Acts 2 there was a clear purpose. The people in Jerusalem and from across the Roman Empire who spoke different languages, heard the gospel in their language and were therefore able to respond. Even in Acts tongues soon became a signifier for more than communicating the gospel to the 'unbeliever', and we find the disciples acknowledging others' legitimacy as believers because they heard them speak in tongues (Acts 10.46). I suspect Pentecostals may never agree among themselves about the place of tongues in the grand scheme of things, and therefore what hope has the wider church of consensus here. But at least the continued practice of this phenomenon in the church acts as a reminder to the whole church of the existential nature of our faith.

Among the many lessons the church might learn from Pentecostals and their emphasis on the gifts of the Spirit, and specifically in regards to speaking in tongues, is one about how best we might speak the languages of the people in our diverse society, particularly the language of the youths of our day. In the same way that the coming of the Holy Spirit in Acts 2 signalled an outbreak of miraculous speech and understanding between speakers and hearers leading to transformation, so too we pray that God would by the Spirit in us enable us to better communicate to young people the wondrous things of God. It is worth reminding ourselves that many believed that the spiritual revival of the late 19th and early 20th century that led to the Pentecostalism we now have, signalled an ability to speak the languages of the peoples of the world and thereby communicate the gospel to them. Missionaries were dispatched from the Azusa Street Mission and its offshoots to China, India and Africa in the belief that they had been empowered to speak the languages of those people having not learned them naturally. Of course they were disappointed to discover that this was not the case. This should have signalled to the church that whilst that was God's modus operandi in Acts 2, it did not signal a method for all time. And so we have to remain open to God in all ages for the means he chooses to use to communicate. What Acts 2 does for me is to raise an awareness of human dependency upon the miraculous to communicate the gospel to those who speak a different 'language' from us. And with so many of today's young people loose and listless in our world, we need that divine intervention more than ever.

ENERGETIC AND DYNAMIC WORSHIP

Something else for which Pentecostals are noted is energetic and dynamic worship. No one likes a dead church service, and Pentecostals in particular don't like silence, sometimes to our cost. I remain unconvinced that cold, purely cerebral worship is enjoyed by many. But the challenge is to bring the energetic worship style of the Pentecostal into contact with the written liturgy of the more formal worship settings. It can work, and some of the more imaginative churches in mainstream Christianity are learning how to mix the well thought through with the spontaneous.

CONCLUSION

Pentecostalism needs saving from becoming increasingly a poor people's expression of faith, by beefing up theologically. So, the significance of Pentecostalism to the ecumenical journey is in part to help us understand the reasons churches that embrace the Pentecostal ethic are growing fast around the world. However, churches in the Pentecostal tradition need to be at the ecumenical table, and cannot afford some spiritual elitism as I believe has happened with Evangelicalism where Evangelical has become a synonym for Christian. But of course, ecumenism is no one thing anymore. As David Spriggs points out in a report for Churches Together in England (CTE), ecumenism happens formally and informally, large scale and small scale, and ecumenical organisations like CTE and the Evangelical Alliance (EA) should never forget that not all that God is doing to bring his church together is channelled through them, significant as they and their God-given work are. So the emphasis on the work of the Holy Spirit being immanent among us may have started with what we have come to call Pentecostalism, but I believe it is a work of and for the whole church. Maybe a good way forward might be for churches to cease from calling themselves Pentecostal, so that Pentecostal can, as I believe God intended, describe the entire living Church of God. There can be no greater significance of Pentecostalism to the ecumenical journey than to share with the whole church what God has shown and done among us. Haste the day of the demise of the Pentecostal church and the rise of the Pentecostalisation of the whole church. Amen!

Lecture to Ecumenical Studies Group, Manchester Cathedral, 26 May 2011

CHAPTER 18

Speaking with one tongue

Tomorrow, Christians celebrate one of our main festivals – Pentecost. This is also known as Whitsunday, or 'White Sunday', depicting how it has become a popular occasion for Christian baptisms where those being baptised wear white.

In churches there will be an atmosphere of celebration with colourfully-robed ministers, symbols of flames and doves, and sermons on themes such as power and the life-giving breath of God.

The Christian festival of Pentecost is rooted in the Jewish festival of Passover. Pentecost means 50, derived from the tradition that the angel of death 'passed over' the Hebrews and destroyed the Egyptian first-born before the flight from Egypt to the Palestinian 'Promised Land'. Fifty days, or seven weeks, after Passover, they celebrated by giving back to God the produce of the fields.

It was for this major Jewish celebration that a first-century gathering in Jerusalem of the disciples of Jesus became what many view as the genesis of the Christian church. Jesus had ascended into heaven and the disciples were waiting for the promise he had made them that God would send them another 'comforter'.

Acts of the Apostles states that suddenly the Holy Spirit came upon them and filled them with spiritual power. There was the sound of a violent wind. Tongues of fire rested upon each of them and they began to speak in languages previously unknown to them, but recognisable to people hearing them.

Birmingham is a city where many languages are spoken, many faiths are embraced, many cultures, ethnicities, nationalities and lifestyles exist. It is a context that cries out for greater understanding. The Christian Pentecost enables us to speak the language of others, sharing with them God's will for our life together.

So, as we gather this Pentecost, may the power of God, through the Holy Spirit, enable us to understand our times, each other and how to respond to the perplexing issues we face together in this city and beyond.

I am one of those who believe that we need divine intervention.

First published in the Birmingham Mail, 2007

Part 6

POLITICS

CHAPTER 19

The church and political engagement

INTRODUCTION

The reason many Christians are anti-politics is because they have a flawed understanding of what politics is. Today I want to share with you some thoughts on the pivotal role of Christians in our community. I believe that when we understand what politics is really about, we will not be afraid of it; indeed we will want to be involved in it as the agents of redemption and transformation that we are under God.

THE MEANING OF POLITICS

Today, in our sceptical society, we tend to be cynical about politics and politicians. So, when we think of the word 'politics' what comes to mind may be closer to what someone called 'polytricks'. That is, we think of the art of trickery, especially as we have come to associate it with Niccolò di Bernardo dei Machiavelli, the 15th and 16th century Italian diplomat, political philosopher, musician, poet and playwright whose name has become synonymous with ruthless politics, deceit and the pursuit of power by any means. The Machiavellian approach to politics conjures up terms such as slight of hand, dishonesty, wheeler-dealer, and so forth. Then, when we think of politicians, this term reminds many of us of such words as crooks, deceivers, people who come round making promises they will wantonly break once they get your vote and get elected.

This is of course not true for everybody. Not all of us are cynical about politics and politicians and not all politicians are Machiavellian. For some of us politics and politicians bring on good, positive vibes as we think of good councillors, MPs, Prime Ministers, or Barack Obama. It is helpful though to go back to first principles in these matters. When we do this we see that the word 'politic' from which we get 'politics' means 'artful', 'shrewd', and 'ingenious'. One meaning of 'politics' conveys "the complex or aggregate of relationships of people in society especially those relationships involving authority and power" (Collins).

One website I visited said this: "Politics is the process by which groups of people make decisions. The term is generally applied to behaviour within civil governments, but politics has been observed in all human group interactions, including corporate, academic, and religious institutions". So, wherever you find people, you will also find politics: attempts to organise, so that decisions can be made in the interest of everyone. Whether at local, national or international level, the artful, the shrewd, the ingenious tend to emerge as political operators and leaders.

SHOULD THE CHURCH BE INVOLVED IN POLITICS?

If politics is not about being devious or looking after number one, but instead is about the well-being of everybody, should the church be involved in politics? By implication there are already political activities occurring in the church. Some inside the church jockey for positions, try to get their family and friends into positions of power and influence, and much besides. Others try to use their corporate power for the benefit of all. Then there are those who are involved in 'community organising' outside of church, in the wider community. What some are afraid of is bad politics that lies and cheats, politics that looks after self-interest and perpetuates nepotism. But the politics that seeks the welfare of people, builds up community and works for the good of all, Christians should be at the forefront of that kind of politics.

We who are called to be the salt of the earth, i.e. its seasoning, its preservative, should not be afraid to help bring justice, peace and redemption to our communities. As light of the world we should bring illumination, clarity and focus on what is good for the benefit of all. In this way we usher in the Kingdom of God which one songwriter says is a kingdom of peace, it's reigning within, and shall ever increase.

In addition to bad politics, some Christians fear party politics. I too cherish my independence which is why I have never joined a political party. However, it is well known that if you want to exercise real power, the most likely way to get elected is as a member of a recognised party. Yes, you lose a bit of autonomy, but you get the backing of a party's political machinery. Non-alignment often condemns you to perpetual protestation, never gaining power. In 1980, Roy Hattersley challenged his Labour Party during their years in the political wilderness to decide whether they wanted to be a party of protest or a party of power. In today's world, if you want to pursue a political career, it seems best to align yourself with a party and work from that party's political base.

POLITICAL ACTION DRIVEN BY MISSION

Politics was different when Jesus walked the earth. There was not the well-developed party political system of today's Britain. However, he remains our best role model for how to do politics. Above all Jesus demonstrated a clarity about his work that we need to understand. Luke, chapter 4 tells us that he had spent forty days and nights in the wilderness being tempted by the devil, being ministered to by angels, and being strengthened by God. After this time of isolation Jesus came out in the power of the Spirit. In the synagogue he read, "the spirit of the Lord is upon me, God has anointed me" (v18). By the time Jesus began his public ministry he was very clear about his mission and about the power behind him.

Jesus' mission was one given him by his Father, and it was nothing short of the total liberation or salvation of mankind. Jesus was about setting people free, and not just for the life to come but for the one right here too. Luke says he became popularly known in Galilee, "news about him spread through the whole region" (v14). For his teaching in the synagogue, "everyone praised him" (v15). Having got people's attention, in the synagogue in Nazareth his hometown, Jesus read his five-point manifesto.

First, good news for the poor (v18) – For those in spiritual and economic deprivation, Jesus has a plan to get you rich!

Second, freedom for prisoners (v18) – For those imprisoned by your captors, in chains to sinful habits, or serving time for crimes committed, Jesus has a plan to set you free.

Third, sight for the blind (v18) – For those who are physically and spiritually blind, cannot see a way beyond your present circumstance, Jesus will restore your sight.

Fourth, liberation for the oppressed (v18) – For those suffering under the heavy load of psychological oppression, in bad relationships, Jesus brings you liberation.

Fifth, divine favour (v19) – For those out of favour with God and man, every turn you make it's like bad luck or 'duppy set pan you', Jesus brings you the year of God's divine favour.

I suggest to us today that this is the kind of political agenda that many are waiting for, and it's the message the church needs to embrace as our mission. We are not here for ourselves, not here to come to church every week selfishly 'for a blessing', NO! We are here to set people free; to go seek them out from under their poverty, from their prison, from their blindness, from their oppression, and from their disfavour – pulling them out of the fire, James said, hating the very garment spotted by flesh. This kind of spiritual politics is much bigger than party politics of course, even if you utilise a party base to work from that is aligned to religious community.

POLITICAL ACTION REQUIRES DISCIPLINE

But, if we are to succeed in the work of the liberation or salvation of the people in the community, we have to organise our personal and communal lives to that end, in a manner we are not at present. Because we care about people, because we have a passion for people, we could set about ensuring we have Christian councillors, Christian MPs, Christian school governors, Christian JP's, etc., who by their presence in the political system and in the judiciary, tilt them in favour of godly principles. We could effectively take over our city for God. We need to have a plan and stick to it. But to get there we need to, like Jesus, become clear about our mission. What is your purpose here? What is my purpose here? What is this church's purpose here? When we can agree that our purpose is not to serve ourselves with endless navel-gazing about how righteous we are, how unrighteous some are, then we can focus upon our mission wholeheartedly.

That mission is to set people free. Having decided that, we need to know who our God-called leaders are and back them, support them with prayer, money and encouragement. 'You feel called to run as a local councillor? I am going to support you.' Whichever party you choose, you should be able to count on the support of your church and the support of individuals in the church. We can do this, yes we can.

CONCLUSION

Should the church be involved in politics? Absolutely yes we should. Yes, we must. Society will be a better place when godly people become the salt and light Jesus says we are. Imagine a local government imbued with Christian principles of love, peace, equity, and a place where justice rolls down like a river. Maybe you have been feeling the call to step out into the area of public life at whatever level: becoming a JP, a school governor, joining a political party, becoming a councillor, an MP, maybe even one day the Prime Minister. Step up to the plate today to make our world a place where Jesus reigns! Yes we can!!

Preached at a local church in Birmingham

Part 7

PREACHING

CHAPTER 20

Preaching today in the Black Pentecostal tradition

INTRODUCTION

Of all the activities that occur in Black Pentecostal churches today, preaching is probably the most noteworthy. It certainly is the activity that commands the biggest allocation of time in any church service.[1] The reason for the centrality of preaching in Black Churches has at least two main roots: one historical, the other biblical. Historically, during the time of plantation slavery, the 'church service' was used as a medium by which to communicate important information such as escape plans; the sermon within the church service as a means of communicating important information continues. These days of course the sermon may be used to communicate things such as dissatisfaction with the status quo and how to handle discrimination at work, still using idioms that are discernable to the insider yet babble to the uninitiated. This is in part what has led African American theologian James Cone to insist that the Black Church started in slavery.[2]

INSPIRE, EDUCATE AND ENTERTAIN

The biblical root of the centrality of preaching in Black Churches is the seriousness with which 2 Timothy 4.2 is embraced as a directive: "preach the Word; be prepared in season and out of season; correct, rebuke and encourage – with great patience and careful instruction" (NIV). Cain Hope Felder describes the message at the heart of this process as "a gospel that disturbs and heals."[3] And today's preachers interpret this as a mandate to inspire, educate and entertain the congregation; through this correction and healing come. Usually, he or she is addressing a people whose forebears arrived in Britain as economic migrants or students, aspirants in search of a better life. They therefore naturally gravitate towards achieving things in life, but often find, in the words of Jimmy Cliff, that there are "many rivers to cross, and I can't seem to find my way over".[4] After a hard week of fighting the good fight of faith, wrestling against principalities and powers, worshipers come to church to be inspired to go out and try again. The preacher must provide inspiration for a people who sing, "up, up, up, I'm going up; you can't keep me down I'm going up".

The Black preacher is also 'edutaining', that is, simultaneously educating and entertaining. Black people living in a predominantly White society have long felt that they are mis-educated and under-educated and that in either event there are things they ought to know which they don't know.[5] In a neo-colonial era, the system is generally believed to conspire to keep them ignorant, as it did during the time of slavery and colonialism. So, who could be more relied upon to educate than the trusted preacher! And the words of the preacher are both those which are found in the Bible, and those found by revelation and observation in the pages of life: the social, economic and political arenas. The preacher also has to entertain a people who because of their historic holiness leanings towards abstinence from everything 'worldly' expect the preacher to sanctify their pent up dance, laughter and a host of other emotions that are brought to the fore in the service, whether by the preacher's eloquence, charisma and inspiration or by some other means.

PINNACLE OF WORSHIP

The significance of preaching in the Black Pentecostal tradition can be easily grasped if one notes that it occupies the place Holy Communion usually does in a 'high-church'. That is, preaching is the highpoint of the church service or as Joel Edwards puts it, "preaching stands at the pinnacle of worship…other activities act as preparatory steps to the altar of the declared word".[6] Indeed, if as Alister McGrath suggests, the term 'sacrament' generally means "an external rite or sign, which in some way conveys grace to believers", then with a little imagination preaching in the Black Pentecostal tradition is best viewed sacramentally.[7] In a very real sense for worshipping listeners the preacher takes them on a journey of inspiration, education, and entertainment that leads them into an encounter with a gracious and forgiving God. The world about them may be unloving, unforgiving and unfunny, but in God's presence there is fullness of joy. This process of 'coming into the presence of God' is understood in this tradition to begin with the 'worship service' and is climaxed by the sermon.

Because preaching is so uniquely important, usually occupying forty minutes to an hour, if the preacher fails to deliver, the whole service will be regarded as having underachieved. This time together in worship has to be understood as the people of God congregating to fellowship with one another and to hear from God, primarily through the 'message' preached by God's 'man of the hour' as he's sometimes called. It is a long awaited moment. As one writer puts it, "...a sermon from God's Word, under the anointing, with the proper flow between preacher and congregation is indeed a thing of sheer beauty".[8] This statement, though from the U.S. context, highlights well its significance and the four key traits of preaching as it occurs within the Black Pentecostal churches in Britain today. Namely, the centrality of the Bible, the significance of being 'anointed', the 'call/response' dynamic between preacher and hearers, and the dilemma of balancing substance and style. This is not the only prism through which it is possible to shed light on preaching in this tradition, but these four foci provide a useful model.

USE OF THE BIBLE

Mark Sturge points out that it is a distinguishing feature of Black Pentecostal churches that the Bible is held in 'very high view'.[9] This also means that preaching in this context requires a thoroughly respectable knowledge of the Scriptures. Often one hears reference to Paul's commendation of Timothy that "from infancy you have known the Holy Scriptures which are able to make you wise for salvation through faith in Christ" (2 Timothy 3.15 NIV). A major reason for the preacher to be thoroughly conversant with the Bible is that the congregation will invariably have a deep acquaintance too. Often as the preacher begins to quote a text, members of the congregation will complete it for the preacher. Care has to be taken though as to how the Bible is used in preaching; it will not go down well if the preacher is too technical, and as a consequence has to stick rigidly to a script. Black preaching therefore tends to be very much literal and action orientated, demanding a literal response of faith and ethical living. To achieve this, the preacher tends towards spiritualising and allegorising the biblical texts.[10] Unfortunately, this method of hermeneutics often occurs at the expense of the historicity and contextual meaning of the text.

What the preacher is appealing to in the Black Pentecostal congregation is a preoccupation, not "with polemical issues like unity, inspiration of scripture and other theological niceties" but the "discovery of something that can be experienced as relevant to their needs", according to Allan Anderson.[11] Black worshippers place a high premium on receiving their 'blessing' and the preacher had better bless the worshipper by inspired Bible preaching, or else! Or else, they may be listening to a different preacher in a different place next week. The Bible, however, is a controversial tool which has been and can be used for good or ill purposes. For example, historically, it is well known that some missionaries have interpreted the Bible in ways so as to make slaves compliant, whilst others have used it for empowerment and liberation of the oppressed. A challenge faced by the preacher then in the Black Pentecostal church is to use the Bible both experientially as a 'life-script' for dealing with present realities as well as a political tool that addresses structural principalities and powers.[12] In Tony Blair-speak, this would be addressing the cause and the cure as in, "tough on crime, tough on the causes of crime".

THE SIGNIFICANCE OF BEING 'ANOINTED'

In the mindset of the Black Pentecostal a key reason why their forefathers broke away from the 'cold and nominal' churches in the late 19th century to form the various holiness churches that spawned the Pentecostal movement was to re-discover the vibrancy and immediacy of the Holy Spirit.[13] Cold cerebral form and language was failing to 'break the yoke' of the human condition of being prisoner to Satan. The preacher needs to transcend his human limitations and be taken over by the Holy Spirit who reads and understands the human condition. This is the anointing often spoken about in Black Pentecostal churches; the power to address the human condition of the downward spiral into sin and sinfulness. Those who come to listen to the preacher have come to find answers to their dilemmas, and those of their families and communities. The preacher needs to be able to read his listeners like a book, tell them where they are and what they need to do, in similar fashion to the happenings on the day of Pentecost that resulted in the question, “Brothers, what shall we do?” (Acts 2.37).

A key challenge for the anointed preacher however is that his audience is for the most part the same audience every week. The task of maintaining a high level of engaged sermonising that delivers something fresh each week is by no means an easy task. The lurch to the ordinary is a constant danger. Some churches counter this by having a number of preachers who take turns to preach each week, with the attendant danger of lack of continuity and standards. It is clear however that the churches that grow tend to be those that accept the challenge of a single preacher who from week to week espouses a vision, expounds the Word of God in keeping with that vision, and invites the congregation to accompany him on his visionary journey to build that congregation and influence the community. If the preacher/pastor takes seriously the God-given anointing to preach good news to the poor, freedom for prisoners, recovery of sight for the blind, release for the oppressed, and proclaim the year of the Lord’s favour (Luke 4.18-19), then there appears to be no end to the number of times the same people will return to hear him “sing them over again to me…wonderful words of life”.

THE ‘CALL/RESPONSE’ DYNAMIC BETWEEN PREACHER AND HEARERS

The Black Pentecostal preacher never preaches alone.[14] Various interactive prompts have been developed, ranging from, ‘tell your neighbour…’, to ‘give your neighbour a high five…’, to ‘you didn’t hear what I just said…’, to ‘I wish I had a worshipping church here today…’, to ‘give me an amen for that…’ All of these and more are aimed at one outcome: generating a response from the listener or what has been called ‘call and response’ preaching. During a sermon that achieves the ‘a thing of sheer beauty’ trademark, people will respond to the preacher in many ways; sometimes doing exactly what the preacher requests, but also with actions of their own, like walking up with their offering for the ‘man of God’, kneeling at the altar to pray, or simply standing in affirmation, sometimes with clenched fist, sometimes with a perpetual nodding of the head.

The practice of listening in silence often observed in British historic churches, including some British Pentecostal churches, is simply not the style in Black Pentecostal churches. If the congregation does not voluntarily respond, the preacher will not permit the silence. Here, silence is not golden, and does not mean consent; it is an insult to the preacher and a clear indication of disagreement and disapproval. And how dare anyone so disrespect God's Word and his anointed vessel, the preacher! However, culture is changing among Black Pentecostals and it is noticeable that as in other areas of culture in transit, such as singing at the graveside, that older Pentecostals are more involved than younger middle class professionals who tend to be more like their stiff upper lip White British counterparts. As Black people become more and more indigenised, it is possible to predict that their churches will become more 'British'. But for the time being, call and response is alive and well in Black Pentecostal churches.

SUBSTANCE VERSUS STYLE

With all the commotion that is at work in the Black Pentecostal churches an obvious question concerns whether this type of preaching is a victory for style over substance.[15] In this regard it is worth pondering why it is that in the British tradition people are rowdy at football matches, yet quiet at cricket matches and in church. Why are we happy to listen to an hour-long political party address or budget speech, but must only have a seven-minute homily in church? Why is it possible to sit for hours in a pub but only one hour in church? Where does substance and style begin and end? Is this a matter of class and culture? Black preachers undeniably spend significant parts of their sermons stylising through repetition or seeking affirmation and other histrionics like long pauses, tongues speaking and rejoicing in dance for example. Given my earlier point that worshippers come to be inspired, educated and entertained, the Black Pentecostal preacher does not have the option to be drab. To attempt to educate without inspiring and entertaining, for example, would lead inexorably to an empty church.

The best of Black Pentecostal preachers spend much time crafting their sermons with clear introduction, central points, and conclusion accompanied by scriptural and experiential references. In the case of one preacher who has built a large congregation, the practice is to spend three days each week working on next Sunday's sermon. This is exceptional, but is also indicative of the significance placed upon the central activity of the Sunday worship experience. The challenge for the Black Pentecostal preacher is to deliver with style a 'message' of substance to inspire this and future generations.[16] No mean feat, and in the best of cases achieved with outstanding results in terms of personal satisfaction for preacher and listener, large following and sums of money and lifestyle to match. However, in many cases sadly, evidence of the one is at the expense of the other; few get it right and yet everyone hopes they are doing God's will.

CONCLUSION

Preaching in the Black Pentecostal tradition then is an immense challenge for all concerned. Preaching is the central component of the Black worship experience which places a heavy responsibility upon the preacher to deliver the word for today, week after week to substantially the same audience. Those who succeed reap rich rewards, but alas! The majority aspire but succeed only partially. Nevertheless, in an imperfect world the preacher is often applauded for attempting to preach the Word of God in an educative, inspirational and entertaining way.

First published in 'The Preacher'

1. See Joe Aldred, *Preaching with Power: Sermons by Black Preachers*, London: Cassall, 1998
2. James H. Cone, Black Theology and Black Power, San Francisco: Harper & Row, 1989, p.91
3. Cain Hope Felder, Troubling Biblical Waters, Maryknoll: Orbis Books, 1989, p.82
4. Jimmy Cliff, The Harder they come, Album and play
5. See *A time to speak*, Paul Grant & Raj Patel, eds., Birmingham: Black Theology Working Group, 1990
6. Joel Edwards, 'The Pulpit Response to Worship' in *Let's Praise Him Again: An African-Caribbean Perspective on Worship*, Kingsway Publication, 1992, pp. 46-66.
7. Alister McGrath, *Christian Theology: An Introduction*, Blackwells, 1994, p.427.

8. N Moore, *Pulpit Confessions*, BSB Publishing Co., 1998, p. 41
9. Mark Sturge, *Look what the Lord has done*, Bible Society, 2005, p.132
10. Joe Aldred and Garnet Parris, The Bible and *the black church' in Bible and Practice*, Chris Rowland and John Vincent Eds. UTU 2001, pp 52-65]
11. Allan Anderson, An Introduction to Pentecostalism, Cambridge University Press, 2004, p. 225
12. Robert Beckford, Dread and Pentecostal: A Political Theology for the Black Church, SPCK, 2000, p.193
13. See Larry Martin, The life and ministry of William J Seymour, Joplin: Christian Life Books, 1999
14. Edwards, Lets Praise Him again
15. See Beckford, Dread and Pentecostalism, chapter 6
16. Sturge, Look what the Lord has done, p. 220

Part 8

MULTICULTURALISM

CHAPTER 21

Multiculturalism is dead – long live multiculturalism

Britain is a multicultural country; if by culture we mean "manners, taste, and intellectual development at a particular time and place", as stated in the Oxford Dictionary. It is indicative of the seriousness we attach to culture that we ascribe the adjective 'cultured' to those who exhibit these qualities in the most refined and developed way. These signifiers, manners, tastes and intellectual prowess are determinants of individual and group cultural identity, distinguishing between insiders and outsiders, and they are entrenched and enforced by a kind of group sub-consciousness. Sometimes this sub-consciousness is driven from the intellectual centres of a group like universities, but at other times they are driven by unknown and unseen yet very real populist cultural powers. At the heart of culture is the question of identity and belonging. Sociologist Paul Gilroy puts it this way, "the distinctive language of identity appears again when people seek to calculate how tacit belonging to a group or community can be transformed into more active styles of solidarity, when they debate where the boundaries around a group should be constituted and how – if at all – they should be enforced. Identity becomes a question of power and authority when a group seeks to realise itself in political form".

Culture is important not for itself, but because the more people that coalesce around a recognised identity the more potential pressure that group can bring to bear upon a particular situation, or the more it can demonstrate to those on the outside how powerful the group with that identity is. In fact I believe that culture with its signifiers of manners, taste and intellectual form becomes exaggerated when it exists within a poly-cultural context. The more diverse the differences the more exaggerated and important each culture needs to be. It's a kind of Darwinian survival of the fittest scenario.

The word in Scripture that best portrays the idea of culture is 'custom', meaning that which is common practice – 'it's what we do round here'. Two good examples of this are found in Judges 11.38-40 and St John 18.39. Even the other form of the use of 'custom', i.e. taxes, is derived from the idea that the tax-gatherer's place of doing business was where everybody came to pay their dues. It's the common behaviour of a group that is custom or culture. Britain is a multicultural society because there are multiple cultures with their signifiers of manners, taste and intellectual norms coexisting within it, competing for recognition, influence and power in the same geographical and social context. But culture exemplified by manners, taste and intellectual type does not operate alone in its context; it is influenced by nationality, for instance.

CULTURE AND NATIONALITY

It is intriguing to see how culture and nationality co-mingle. There is little doubt for example that the Welsh, Irish, Scottish and English have both some cultural continuities and discontinuities. I work in national ecumenism, and have been struck by the difference in manners, taste and intellectual type as I go from one country to another within Britain and Ireland. What churches do, how they do it and the vocabulary they use differ from one place to another. But cultural continuities and discontinuities go deeper, so that there are differences in Wales between how things are run in Cardiff as distinct from Swansea. We find similar differentials between say London or Birmingham or Manchester cultures. But then we find that a church may transcend nationality in their cultural behaviour, so that a church in Edinburgh may have more in common with another in London than one in Glasgow because of the denominational culture that remains truer to the historicity of the denomination than to particular national religious norms. And you don't need me to tell you that haggis is not as popular in Wales as it is in Scotland.

Which takes me to some differentials that have their roots in nationalities outside of the UK. I was born in Jamaica, and to me for a long time the difference between a Scotsman, a Welshman, an Irishman and an Englishman was insignificant, if it existed at all; they were all White men – all the same. They all like fish and chips, or so I thought. Unlike them, I am Black, like rice and peas and chicken, ackee and salt fish, and some of my wilder friends like 110% proof white rum,

Red Stripe beer, and we all like Blue Mountain coffee. But having lived here for a while, I now have a British as well as a Jamaican passport and I meet more and more White people who have spent far more time in Africa than I have, understand much more about African cultures than I do. I meet more and more White folks who know Jamaica better than I, know more about Jamaica ire and ital, and Bob Marley than I do. I even discovered that Bob Marley is mixed race and his father is a Scotsman! And like me there are many in Britain today who have nationalities and cultures that are hybrid and different particularly because they come not from Wales, Ireland, Scotland or England, but from further afield.

But of course many of the people living in Britain today within this cultural polyglot hail from countries that consider themselves quite British. In fact, as Yasmin Alibhai-Brown points out, a high percentage of the people living here today are here precisely because Britain went to them in the first place and in its empire building days exported British culture to those lands and peoples. And one of the amusing cultural anecdotes is the way in which British culture in Britain has continued to evolve whilst the places to which it was taken have tended to hold on to it pretty much as they received it. This is so not least because British culture was not just taken to foreign lands, it was generally imposed upon people thought inferior. In the colonisers' mind good was being done by repudiating and forbidding the practice of native cultures in favour of the much more civilised and enlightened cultural idioms evident in the manners, tastes and intellectual norms brought by the benevolent masters. Imagine the sheer disorientation of those people who coming to what they thought was the 'motherland' of good manners, cultured tastes and intellectual prowess, to encounter coarseness, ignorance and racial bigotry.

CULTURE, RACE AND ETHNICITY

The interface between manners, taste and intellect on the one hand, and race or ethnicity on the other, is an interesting one. I recall well reading for the first time Ivan Hannaford's book 'Race – The history of an idea in the West'. Hannaford makes the case that the concept of 'race' as a means by which to categorise the human species is a flawed concept developed in the West to legitimise its treatment of non-western peoples, e.g. Black people. In this perverse intersection, non-western cultures are seen by westerners almost exclusively through the prism of race and ethnicity, what Hannaford calls "blood and belonging", rather than through manners, tastes and intellect. Basically, if it emanates from certain quarters it is intrinsically inadequate; no need to waste time scrutinising it, it's worthless. Most good liberal people today would not wish to associate themselves with such ignorant dismissing of other cultures; in fact we are very keen to promote the notion that we all have something to learn from each other. Quite right too. However, for those of us who come from other parts of the world it's not hard to detect the fault line here, evident sometimes in a certain kind of overcompensation. There are also clear cases of rejection of the 'other' based on little more than racialised stereotyping.

We see this graphically illustrated in the manner in which White British Christians reacted to Black Christians coming into Britain since the 1950s. In my book 'Respect – Understanding Caribbean British Christianity' I quote Bishop Ron Brown, former national leader of the New Testament Church of God in this country, reflecting upon how in those early days the churches brought by people from the Caribbean and planted here were called universally 'sects'. Bishop Brown goes on to muse upon how today these same churches are part of the mainstream of British Christianity. Indeed, they constitute the rare thriving element of British Christianity. But they were met with what has been widely cited by many Caribbean British writers who experienced it as cold a welcome as the British weather in winter. However, what they brought is now the stuff by which the church survives and grows.

There is a real struggle to make healthy the relationship between culture, race and ethnicity. And of course the place to start is with the understanding that whatever our culture, race or ethnicity we are first and foremost human beings made in the image and likeness of God. As though our common humanity were not enough, as Christians we also share the one faith and baptism of the one catholic church. When this is understood and becomes our modus vivendi, we immediately recognise that the God in whose image we are made and whose likeness we share and who is no respecter of persons has endued us all with the abilities to develop appropriate cultures. These cultures are contextual and our approach should always be one of respectful inquiry, leading to better appreciation of the 'other'. This leads to sharing in the richness of God's creative diversity, seeing no culture as superior or inferior, all legitimised by our human godlikeness. Or as Bhikhu Parekh suggests, since each culture represents a distinct way of life, it needs to be approached with sensitivity and empathy and calls for great powers of imagination (p77, Rethinking Multiculturalism).

An aspect of our multicultural existence in Britain that I ought to say something further about is the manner in which multiculturalism has become an industry overtaken by ideology and funding. Ideologically, we vacillate between a kind of cultural 'moral monism' as Bhikhu Parekh calls it, and cultural plurality. There appears to be an unease with accepting that we humans can be simultaneously different and the same, and that we don't have to choose between one and the other. So ideologically we are driven by political and popular waves of perceptions of what for example it means to be British, or worse, English. And in any case, who decides what this means? Norman Tebbit, with his 'cricket test'? Or me, who feels quite at ease to call myself Caribbean British, and support the West Indies cricket team when they play anybody, including England; but then turn and support England when we play anybody apart from the West Indies? Because we cannot agree whether culture is homogenised or pluralist, we have become schizophrenic in our attitude towards diversity. One day we are for multiculturalism, the next day we are not.

Recently, the Chair of the CRE, Trevor Phillips, called for us to move beyond multiculturalism. I asked him in person what he meant. I understood by his reply that he is keen to move beyond the idea of multiculturalism as something that simply reinforces difference rather than promotes unity. I agree with him. What is not clear however, is whether Phillips' idea of cultural unity is a unity around an artificial notion of Britishness that calls for the abandonment of other cultural norms. My own opinion, for what it's worth, is that this is a flawed choice that we are called upon to make. What is required in my view is better understanding of self and the other, and an active participating in the cultural life of the other. As we do so, we grow in our appreciation of what it is we both like and dislike about our own culture and what it is that we both like and dislike about the culture of our neighbour. What then binds us together is security in our difference as well as those things that we end up sharing. This kind of organic process may still have room for an industry that promotes better understanding but would be bereft of the competitive funding rounds that force individuals and organisations to emphasise difference and polarities as justification for why they need funding. Indeed we may be moving in the right direction by the emerging requirements for government funding to demonstrate that any project from a particular cultural grouping will involve at least one other cultural or ethnic group. Plurality and diversity that is under-girded by education and information has got to be a better way than forcing everybody into contrived notions of a homogeneous British identity.

MULTICULTURAL CHURCH

The cultural dilemma is reflected in our relationships in the church in Britain too. As an ecumenist travelling across this country and across denominations I find it wonderfully bewildering and enriching at the same time to make sense of the different cultural leanings of the churches. This means for example, that something I say in one church culture is viewed as liberal, whilst the same thing said in another setting marks me out as conservative. Equally, I have to moderate my preaching style in terms of length and content depending upon where in the church in Britain I am. I have become accustomed to this way of working, although I have to admit it is sometimes tiring. Wouldn't it be easier if the church were the same everywhere and I could just slip in and out of one place and another without changing gear? My answer is, 'no'. What a boring place that would be.

The multiplicity of denominations may not be ideal, but I for one believe that if we did not have denominations we would invent them. When John in Revelation saw the great multitude he could not count in heaven, they were from every tribe, people and language (Revelation 7.9). This may be poor exegesis but I take this to mean that not only does God make diversity in plant life, but in human life and in our spiritual life too. So rather than get hung up on our difference in the denominations, I prefer to see this as variety to be challenged by whilst also focussing upon our commonalities. In the same way that humans are simultaneously the same and different, so too are our churches. Isn't it amusing how it is that as humans there really are basically two types of us: male and female. Yet all 3 billion males spend our time hiding from each other or showing off as though the body parts we have are peculiar to us. I guess women do the same. Substantially we are the same. And yet we spend so much energy either pretending we are different, or failing to share our real differences. As I traverse churches, Black Churches, I was initially amazed at the number that believe that they are the only true church. I had thought that was the teaching of my denomination alone. No, all of us in our small corner are claiming the same thing. Now if we all got together, we would soon discover the fallacy of that claim and spend our time together and apart doing more useful things.

God's church is a multicultural church, a rainbow church, in which if we could conceive a better notion of who we are, we might add the violet to the indigo to the blue to the green to the yellow to the orange to the red to become the rainbow people of God assuring the world that the day of redemption is here. "By this," Jesus said, "the world will know that you are my disciples, when you have love one for the other." This takes me to what I am calling a theology of working together, that the world may believe.

A THEOLOGY OF WORKING TOGETHER

When I was a young man we used to sing in the churches a little song: "come let us pull, pull, pull all together". And there is a maxim that says, 'united we stand, divided we fall'. The challenge to the church in our day, the same as challenges society as a whole, is whether we can get beyond the rhetoric about unity and get to practical cooperation in mission. In my other two talks I will look first, at how dealing with the legacies of the Slave Trade we might find ways of moving forward together as descendants of slave masters and slaves, and second, at how a better understanding of the Holy Spirit might also lead to better working relationships. But here, let me look at a theological basis for working together. The prize is fantastic. If we can overcome all our historic, social, political and theological differences and work together there surely must be a God in heaven. However, the cost of failure to work together is catastrophic. Divided, we fall.

I am interested to note Jesus' perspective on the functional unity he shares with his Father and the Holy Spirit. It begins with Jesus' assertion that everything he did was with his Father's expressed will and permission. And that He and the Father were one. Jesus' unity with the Father gave both validity and authority to his missiological acts. He did nothing in his own name but in the Father's name alone. His selflessness and constant allusion to the Father so irritated and bemused people that they demanded, "show us the Father". Then came Jesus' irritating response, "if you have seen me, you have seen the Father". Here's my tease; what would it be like if we as individual Christians and churches were to refuse to do anything in our own name, and found legitimacy for our actions only in that we were doing the will of God for the benefit of another? How much of what you do is for you, your family, your church? How many truly altruistic activities do you engage in a day, a week, a month, a year? Is it not the case that we are tied up in knots by our own needs and the demands of our churches? So much so that ministries that were vibrant have now become a drudgery, slave-like in their manner of operation and existence?

In the past two months, I have come across two young men both tired of the exclusive nature of the requirements and demands of their denominations. Feeling the need to break free, one has left the restricting framework of his denomination; the other has now engaged in an elaborate scheme of librating the local expression of his church from its oppressive headquarters. In both cases my response is what a waste of energy. Necessary as both may feel their actions are, it seems to me like misdirected energies at a time when the world stands there and says convince me about your claims that there is a saviour in Jesus Christ. A recent survey has apparently shown that millions of non-church going people in this country would go to church if asked, but who is asking? Not that going to church equates with being Christian, but at a time when 70% of us say we believe in God and only 6% go to church, there is clearly lots of work to do in mission and evangelism.

It is my view that the manner in which our situation is best tackled is in the Jesus way of unity. "Father", he prayed, "make them one as we are one" (St John 17). This Trinitarian oneness is a template for our oneness. I believe we have to join forces in our oneness as Christians across artificial denominational, cultural, national, ethnic and racial lines to impact an unbelieving world. We can utilise our God-given difference and the innate qualities with which God has imbued this difference to reach the world with the message of the gospel of Jesus Christ. Foolishly, I believe that God has placed all we need to do and what we need to do in the world within the church already. What hampers us is that instead of using the walls between us to move up higher we use them as dividers only, and so lock ourselves away from each other with our gifts and talents. As we bring into play all the gifts and talents and cultures and nationalities and ethnicities into the service of the other under the direction of God, I believe we are getting somewhere close to God's heart for his mission through us on earth.

CONCLUSION

So let me conclude by restating that it's not multiculturalism that we need to kill off, either in the world or in the church; variety really is the God-given spice of life. What is needed is a greater appreciation of our own culture and those of others. What is needed too is a commitment to unity in diversity that respects what we share in common as well as what we hold dear but different.

Talk delivered to Eastern Ecumenical Training Course

Part 9

CHRISTMAS

CHAPTER 22

God's greatest gift

St John 3.1-21. Verse 16, "For God so loved the world that he gave his one and only Son, that whoever believes in him shall not perish but have eternal life" (NIV).

My sermon today focuses on a well-known text that has been our Golden Text or Memory Verse many, many times. Most of those of us who know it, will have memorised it in the 17th century English of the Authorised King James Version of the Bible. Let's say it together from there: "For God so loved the world that he gave his only begotten Son, that whosoever believeth on him, should not perish but have everlasting life". The New International Version renders it: "For God so loved the world that he gave his one and only Son, that whoever believes in him shall not perish but have eternal life".

In whatever version, the message remains the same: first, God loves the world; second, God has given a very special gift to the world; and third, whoever believes or has faith in what God has given has eternal life. And it is these three thoughts that I share with you today in this sermon.

But first, allow me to set this verse within the context that it is brought to us in the Scriptures. The book of John is often referred to as the fourth Gospel, after Matthew, Mark and Luke. It is believed by some to have been completed during the last decade of the first century AD. And as not every book of the Bible that bears a person's name is written by the person whose name it bears, so the fourth gospel is reckoned by most scholars to have been written by a Johannine community which traced its traditions back to the apostle John, the son of Zebedee. This is the John who is referred to in Scripture as the "beloved disciple". It was this John that Jesus, while on the cross, instructed to take care of his mother Mary. It becomes clear from this Gospel that its 'writer' had a close relationship with and understanding of Jesus.

It is not surprising therefore that even after the other three Evangelists Matthew, Mark and Luke had written their accounts, John's followers had a determination to write his own account of matters relating to the life of the Jesus he had come to know and love. Their objective is very clear: in the Gospel according to John, Jesus is portrayed as the Incarnate Son of God; the Christ; the Messiah. John portrays Jesus as what one writer calls, "the unique Son of God". Clement of Alexandra, a Christian apologist, missionary theologian to the Greek cultural world in the late 2nd century and early 3rd century, described the Gospel of John as the "spiritual Gospel", because of its extensive portrayal of the divine revelation of Jesus as the Eternal Son of God. And even today, when we as pastors and teachers want to ground a new Christian in the faith of Jesus Christ as God revealed to humanity, it is to the Gospel of John that we point. If you haven't read it yet, I encourage you to do so at your earliest convenience.

It is in the third chapter of this inspirational Gospel of John that we find our text that we know so well. Here, Jesus, the central figure of John, has a meeting with a man by the name of Nicodemus. We learn from the text that Nicodemus was a member of the Jewish sect called the Pharisees, and he was a member of the ruling Sanhedrin Council which was in opposition to Jesus. But Nicodemus was intrigued, curious – how can a man, any man, do the miracles Jesus of Nazareth was doing unless God was with and in him? Nicodemus wanted to find out more, but he had a problem. He was part of the religious government of Israel where as far as he knew everybody viewed Jesus as a threat, so he could hardly be seen cosying up to the opposition.

Nicodemus decided to go under cover. He went to Jesus at night, away from the glare and condemnation of his colleagues. Let me pause a moment to speak to somebody here today. You may have a curiosity about the things of God, but present company and circumstance do not make it easy. You feel guilty, between a rock and a hard place: God is calling, but what will your friends and colleagues who are intelligent or in high society think? Well, take a leaf out of Nicodemus' book. You don't always have to jump in with both feet, or wear your Christianity on your sleeve; sometimes you might be better off slipping out the back door to go and find out. May be that's how you come to be here today! Well done!! You never know where this inauspicious beginning might lead.

Nicodemus didn't do too badly with his quiet diplomatic form of Christianity. He may have started under cover of darkness, but John reminds us that later when Jesus came before the religious court, the Sanhedrin, of which Nicodemus was a member, it was he who spoke up asking rhetorically, "does our law condemn a man without first hearing him to find out what he is doing?" (St John 7.52). Then after Jesus' death it was Nicodemus along with another secret follower, Joseph of Aramathea (no relation), who with Pilate's permission took Jesus' body and covered it in myrrh, aloes, spices and linen as was the custom of the Jews, and buried him in some kind of dignity (St John 19.39-42). Nicodemus and Joseph of Aramathea show us that God does not always want us to leave where we are. Maybe you work in a profession or a place that people would ridicule you if they knew you were a professing Christian. God still can use you right there under cover.

So, back to Nicodemus and Jesus on the night of encounter that led up to St John 3.16. Imagine Nicodemus, a little scared, not sure if he was being followed, apprehensive about meeting Jesus probably for the first time. You know how it is at moments like this, you just don't really know what to say. He begins with a compliment: "Rabbi, we know you are a teacher who has come from God. For no one could perform the miraculous signs you are doing if God were not with him" (v2).

This I have to tell you is one of my favourite exchanges in Scripture. Most of us would have been so lost in the flattery of the compliment, we would lose our senses, go all wobbly at the knees as our head swells. But Jesus, the Son of God who is so unlike us in that way, brushing aside Nicodemus' attempt at complimenting him, got right to the heart of the matter! He says to Nicodemus, "I tell you the truth, unless a man is born again," (properly translated, this means 'born from above') "he cannot see the kingdom of God" (v3). Now, there's a conversation stopper! Jesus' response was hardly a direct answer to Nicodemus' statement. At times we think that we have to say just the right words, but Jesus shows that sometimes the right words are not the ones that correctly follow the human sequence of the conversation.

You can read the rest of that story in the ensuing verses, but here is what is at the heart of this sermon. Never mind all the miraculous signs and wonders that send shivers down your spine; never mind how many times your body gets healed; never mind how many times manna falls from the sky and save your natural life; Nicodemus, Freda, Bobby, Samuel, or whatever your name is, the important thing is that you need to be born again, from above. Why? Because you along with the rest of the human race have fallen in the decadence of sin and are on the wrong side of God.

Like Nicodemus we are so prone to follow signs, whether those are our star signs or others. None of those will give us the new life we need if we are to live as God intended when he created us in his divine image. God has a plan to restore you and I back to that place of spiritual existence that he always intended for us, when, as the Bible puts it, he walked with Adam and Eve in the Garden of Eden in the cool of the day. Maybe today, your life is just a material one, lived in the grip of scientific materialism without reference to the Almighty Creator who made you in His image and likeness. God is calling and confronting you like Jesus did with Nicodemus. You may be saying all kinds of things, babbling away about how good God is, life is, the job is, friends are but Jesus is simply saying never mind all that, how is your spiritual life?

But God also knows that you cannot fix up yourself by yourself. So, here are three things we need to know from St John 3.16, lessons from Jesus' encounter with Nicodemus. First, God loves the world and that includes YOU. Let's look briefly in turn at 'God', 'love' and 'the world'. The God to whom I refer today is the Creator of us and everything that exists, visible and invisible. We did not create ourselves. You did not make you, therefore you have to ask yourself, who made me, and why? What's God's purpose? What's my destiny?

The love that is referred to here is a special kind of emotion. It comes from the Greek word Agape and means an unconditional state of fondness, acceptance and care. Last week, a preacher said we were worm. Well, the Bible alludes to this, but only in the sense of our sinful condition. In our proper state of righteousness to which God wants to restore us, we are what theologians call the 'imago dei' i.e. the dead stamp of God! – as we say in Jamaica. And that ain't no worm.

The world that is mentioned is the cosmos. The Creator loves the entire creation. If God loves the moon and the stars and the earth, guess what he thinks of you and me who reflect his image and glory.

God loves all of humanity, whatever your colour, ethnicity, nationality or tribe. God loves you even while your life is upside down and in a mess. God loves you not because of your condition, but because you are his handmade! You are part of his creation, his world. He loves you.

The second theme in St John 3.16 is this: God the Creator of the universe, has given a very special gift to the world. Some of us will recall that little chorus, "all good gifts around us are sent from heaven above…" That reminds us that there are many gifts that God gives us, and they are all good. But there is one gift that is above all others! That's why this month this church is focussing on the theme of 'God's greatest gift'. A gift is something you part with unconditionally and is received unconditionally. A gift cannot be worked for, and we should not attach demands to our giving of gifts. It is like the brata you get in the Spanish Town market when you buy a dozen mangoes and the 'iggler' woman gives you an extra one you didn't pay for. But this is more than mango and neesberries and breadfruit. Sometimes we get gifts we don't need and never use, or maybe use once and never again. Most gifts we get are near worthless, or at best temporary.

But God's gift to us is the very thing we need to restore us back to peace with God; this gift is his One and Only Son. This is why Nicodemus' flattery got short shrift – Jesus was really saying, "my miraculous signs count for nothing if they don't point you to your need for spiritual renewal". And when you see that need, you will understand the purpose of God's gift in Jesus Christ. Jesus' mission, and mine today, is to point you to God's greatest gift. John says of Jesus, "He was in the beginning with God; He was with God and was God. All things were made by him and without him was nothing made that was made. He came to his own but they did not recognise him. He didn't just appear in Mary's womb; he was alive with God as the Logos, the living Word of God in creation. This is why he is such a Great gift, because he created you and knows you; your uprising and your down sitting; your struggles and your joys; your ambitions and your needs; your achievements and your disappointments. God in Jesus knows you more than you know yourself.

When the Bible speaks of the only begotten of the father, this is not a cry for sympathy as would be the case if you or I had an only child and gave him or her up to be crucified. This is the one and only divine eternally existent Son of Creator God. He is special because he comes from God, a unique pre and post historical figure who is, in fact, God's own self. Isaiah allegorises about him in this way: "For unto us a child is born, to us a son is given, and the government will be on his shoulders. And he will be called Wonderful, Counsellor, Mighty God, Everlasting Father, Prince of Peace" (Isaiah 9.6).

The third theme in St John 3.16 is that whoever believes in Jesus, God gives you eternal life. Whoever simply means whoever! It means that it matters not what nationality you are, what colour you are, what gender you are, whether you are rich or poor, educated or illiterate: if you believe in Jesus you have eternal life. But what does it mean to believe in Jesus? It certainly does not mean believing in or belonging to a church or club or any thing else. To believe in Jesus is to accept that the pre-existent Word or Logos became the Incarnate God-man who was born in Palestine 2000 years ago who lived, performed miracles, was without sin, yet was betrayed and condemned to death by hanging, he who died and rose again by God's miraculous power was and is indeed God's own self.

This faith, this belief in Jesus, God's Son who lived and died, gives you and me eternal life. The old King James version of the Bible uses the term 'everlasting life' which tends to focus on living forever as a result of having faith in Jesus. However, newer translations more appropriately focus on 'eternal' life, instead of 'everlasting' life. This is not to say there is no everlasting life, but God wants those of us who are his children to not wait to really live life to the full when we 'get over yonder'; God wants you to live life to the full in the here and now. Jesus says to us, "I have come that you may have life and live it in its fullness". Eternal life speaks of the quality of life more so than its length. You see, you can live a long and miserable life, and that's not what God desires for you. As we understand hell, people there will live everlastingly, but nobody wants to be there. Eternal life, quality living, begins here the moment you and I accept Jesus as our Lord and Saviour.

So St John 3.16 focuses our minds on the greatest gift God has to offer. This Christmas, amidst the many gifts you give and receive the greatest one of all is Jesus who came from God, became one of us, died for us and now offers us remission for all our sin at the cost only of having faith in his finished work on the cross of Calvary. Amen.

Part 10

MONEY

CHAPTER 23

The sin of simony – a threat to the poor and vulnerable

The term 'sin of simony' describes the incident in the Scriptures where Simon the sorcerer tried, unsuccessfully, to buy the miraculous power of God that he witnessed in the apostles. Analogies can be misleading, but sometimes their poignancy helps to concentrate the mind. Such is the case in making the 'prosperity gospel' analogous of the 'Sin of Simony'.

The background to the text in Acts chapter 8 concerns the Samaritans who were regarded as impure and therefore excluded by so-called pure Jews. The Jewish returnees from Babylonian exile made Jerusalem their place of worship, free from the syncretistic religious practices of the Samaritans. The division between Jews and Samaritans is illustrated in the famed story of the 'woman at the well' (St John 4). The woman reminded Jesus, "you are a Jew and I am a Samaritan woman. How can you ask me for a drink?" The Jews do not associate with Samaritans, the scribe helpfully adds.

So it was to these excluded people that the apostle Philip and others brought the wonderful message of a new gospel of equality and inclusion through Jesus Christ. And to validate the veracity of the new message, God accompanied their preaching with miraculous signs and wonders. The Samaritans loved what they were hearing and experiencing and flocked to hear more. There was great joy in the city of Samaria! But not everybody was rejoicing.

Simon who made a living by bewitching the people with his sorcery, his slight of hand, realised that this new message of free access to God and God's power of deliverance threatened his livelihood. He knew the people would not continue to pay him for his counterfeit miracles once they realised that he was merely bamboozling them by clever magic, and at a high price!

Sensing the impending economic crunch, Simon first sought alignment with the apostles and got baptised. Reminding us of a line in a John Legend song where in order to get his girl he promised to "get baptised" if he had to. Simon offered the apostles money to buy the power they were demonstrating for free, so he could sell it. Peter's response was simple, "your money perish with you… go repent of your wickedness". This is the background to the sin of simony.

I have become concerned about preachers who tell their captive audience to 'sow' money into their ministry and the Lord will bless the giver tenfold, saying 'your miracle is in your giving', or similar sounding phrases. The audience, whether TV viewers or a church congregation, will almost always include people feeling the need for 'a miracle', and whereas the apostles dispensed their power for free, today many are putting a price on your blessing. And they do not want loose change either! When someone struggling to get out of debt, or praying for healing from a life-threatening illness hear a 'man or woman of God' say sow a financial seed into my ministry and expect a miracle, the desperate listener is put between a rock and a hard place. Instinct is to obey the man or woman of God!

Recently I witnessed a financial collection in a church meeting by an international speaker. I turned to a young woman I knew standing near me and asked, "aren't you going up with your £1,000 to receive your miracle?" She responded, "I'm still paying off the last £1,000 I pledged!"

As I write I am aware that there are many who have been made more destitute by the demands of prosperity preachers who have 'persuaded' them that the way out of their predicament is to part with money – money they don't really have and some even borrow. Is this the sin of simony? You decide. What I am clear about is that I know of no account in Jesus' ministry linking money to miracles.

At this point some may wish to refer me to the book of Malachi and the injunction to "bring all the tithes into my storehouse and see if I will not pour you out a blessing you will not have room to contain". Well, that is a lovely Old Testament text which at another time I am happy to explore. But for now, allow me to point out that the New Testament offers those who turn to God, life in all its fullness, without putting a price tag on such prospering. And whilst acknowledging that the workman is worthy of his due, and God loves a cheerful giver, the only legitimate biblical link between miracle and money is that both words begin with the letter 'm'.

The poor and vulnerable should be supported, never exploited. The sin of simony has no place in the church of Jesus Christ. Freely we have received, freely give. Ministries need financial support, but not by spiritual or emotional blackmail!

Part 11

LEADERSHIP

CHAPTER 24

Lessons from Esther

Text: Esther 4.14 "For if you keep silence at such a time as this, relief and deliverance will rise for the Jews from another quarter, but you and your father's family will perish. Who knows? Perhaps you have come to royal dignity for just such a time as this" (NRSV).

INTRODUCTION

This well-known phrase, "Who knows? Perhaps you have come to the kingdom for just such a time as this," speaks of the dilemma Esther faced as a woman of a minority culture, in a male dominated society, and the stark reality that having come into prominence she needed to use the position not just for her own personal comfort and safety, but for the liberation of her oppressed people and to the glory of God.

The book of Esther is a fascinating book that tells the story of how the Jews, scattered abroad in the Diaspora of a Persian Empire that was centred in modern day Iran and stretched from India in the east to Africa in the west, faced total annihilation because of trumped up charges; how they were miraculously spared by the courage and enterprise of Esther and her uncle Mordecai. The book is fascinating too for other reasons. It's a West Indian book because some of the people in it have more than one name! The king has two near unpronounceable names: Ahasuerus and Xerxes. Esther, which means 'a star', is the Persian name of our main character whose Hebrew name is Hadassah, meaning a Myrtle tree; so if we wanted to we could call her Miss Myrtle! Another reason that you may find the book of Esther interesting is that there are two versions of it. The one in the Protestant Bible doesn't actually mention the word God, even though we can discern God's providence in it. Yet the other version in what Jamaicans call the Macabees, does. Growing up in Jamaica, I was always told by the Rastafarians that we don't have the right Bible, because the right Bible that the White people have, has the Macabees in it. Of course the Apocryphal or Deutero-canonical books are more than the Macabees, and include this other version of Esther. When I read it I do wonder if the compilers of the Protestant Bible left the wrong version in. If you don't have it already, get yourself a Bible with the Apocryphal books and read the two versions of Esther for yourself and see what I mean.

There are three key points I want to share with us today from this wonderful book of Esther which I am encouraging you to go and read in both versions.

FIRST, IT'S A MAN'S WORLD

Esther lived in a male dominated world where the woman was little more than his decoration. She discovered what many of us know today, that the challenges faced by minorities are multi-layered and that even in a man's world, some men are greater than other men, and some women prosper more than and sometimes at the expense of other women. So we see that when the king promoted a man named Haman to be his second in command, everybody, both men and women were expected to bow to him. When Mordecai refused because of his faith that told him not to bow to any other god but the true and living God, he so annoyed Haman that he couldn't sleep and plotted to kill him, making a gallows to hang him on, but upon which in the end he himself was hanged – remember the Caribbean saying that when you dig a hole for your enemy, dig two; so when you make a gallows for someone else remember that it may well be you who hang on it. It was a man's world and yet when Queen Vashti refused, having been ordered to appear before the drunken king who wanted to show her off and parade her before his visiting subordinate nobles and governors from his vast empire of 27 provinces, her demise was the opening for Esther to be spotted as replacement queen. Indeed it was such a man's world that Queen Vashti's feistiness in refusing to go to her husband was said to be a threat to all men, since when women throughout the empire would hear that the queen refused to obey her husband the king, that would embolden them to disobey and dishonour all the husbands in the empire. A decree was sent to all parts of the empire to every people and language that every man, high or low, must be master in his own house (Esther 1.22). Here we see both the power of a woman and the vulnerability and insecurity of men. But Esther and the thousands of beautiful women who were recruited as prospects to replace Vashti as queen did not follow Vashti's brave stance, but instead jumped at the chance to be queen in her stead. Dorothy, you come to this job in a man's world with all these relationship complications.

My second lesson from the book of Esther is that she had patience and tact. The process for selection of a queen to replace Vashti took a long time. The whole realm was scoured for all the most beautiful virgins to be gathered in the king's harem under the watchful eyes of eunuchs, with their sex drives removed; the virgins were to be treated with the best cosmetics and after a year or so, the best seven would appear before the king. Throughout this process Esther aided and abetted by her uncle Mordecai kept her cool and said nothing about her ethnicity. Had it been known that she was a Jewess, no doubt she would have been excluded from the beauty contest. Her uncle advised her to keep that quiet. Then later when she had the chance to request anything she wanted from the king, she bided her time, didn't rush in as we are often tempted to do before the offer comes out of the mouth. She waited for Haman's vile plan to hang Mordicai, for his insubordination to unravel as he told the king what should be done for the man who had uncovered a plot to kill the king, not realising that it was not him the king was seeking to reward and promote, but Mordecai for whom Haman had built the gallows. It pays to be calm even in times of great danger and distress; let your enemies' plans come to their fateful end; let their plots against you unravel themselves because of their inherent unrighteousness; let God deliver them into their own deserved dead end. We must learn like Esther to stand still and see the salvation of the Lord!

And third, we learn from the book of Esther that personal promotion or prominence is for a purpose, not for selfish ends. Having become queen in place of Vashti, Esther now sits comfortable in the splendour of the Citadel of Susa. Her life of poverty and as an ethnic minority now replaced by being queen in the Persian Empire. She took some persuading to join the plan to save her people. Mordecai had to remind her not to think that she was safe simply because she had now acceded to her high place next to the king as queen. In fact her vulnerability is in part explained when we read that for thirty days she had not been called before the king – he had many more beautiful women and possible replacements in his harem. Esther eventually got with the programme; she fasted and decided to risk all to save her people with whom her destiny was clearly wrapped up. Esther agreed to risk appearing before the king even though he hadn't called for her; she knew that if he didn't raise his royal sceptre once she appeared in his court, she was a dead woman. But she knew that if she didn't take the risk, she was in danger anyway. She was in favour and you can read the whole story in the book of Esther. So the message is clear, we don't get to prominence to play safe. In the end because of Esther, the star's bravery and commitment to her people, the royal decree to wipe out the Jews was reversed; Haman who conceived the plan was hanged with his sons on the gallows he made; Mordecai was able to replace his sackcloth and ashes with royal robes as second in command to the King and Esther's position as queen was enhanced. Her risk taking paid off. So Reverend Rose, star, take risks in pursuit of your divine destiny, seek after God's will and as long as you are in this position, never lose sight of the needs of the people of whom you are an interwoven part.

These lessons from Esther still challenge us today with that question, "Who knows? Perhaps you have come to the kingdom, to prominence, for such a time as this?"

Address at the installation of Revd Dorothy Rose as pastor of Hampstead Road Baptist Church

CHAPTER 25

The big picture (Genesis 12.1-9 & St John 4.31-38)

INTRODUCTION

I begin with this well known quote from the late Aiden Wilson (AW) Tozer: "The history of mankind will probably show that no people has ever risen above its religion, and no religion has ever been greater than its idea of God". This statement is so profound. There was a time when it was felt that religion, in particular the Christian faith, was a driver for progress. Things changed with the European Enlightenment of the 18th century that prioritised reason and science and intellectual interchange. The Enlightenment viewed the non scientific as superstition and therefore unworthy of the modern thinking person. Up to the Enlightenment when faith held sway in Europe, intelligent people generally aspired to be vicars and bishops and theologians before philosopher, doctor, teacher. The church was powerful and if you wanted to get ahead you got into religion. But with the Enlightenment has come every conceivable attempt to undermine religion as superstitious nonsense. And since a nation cannot rise higher than the strong force of its religion, the likes of atheist Richard Dawkins says religion must be purged from the face of the earth, so that people can rise to their full potential without religion inhibiting them.

However, religion's problem is not just that unbelievers are champing at the bit to cut it down – and they've been trying with works like the *Death of God*, *God is not Great*, *The Da Vinci Code*, *The God Delusion*, *The Devil's Vicar* and many more. The bigger threat to religion, in my view, concerns the second part of Tozer's hypothesis: that a religion cannot rise above its idea of God. The challenge of the modern pastor is not just to give the faithful an emotional high in church every Sunday, or to make them feel guilty and dependent upon them. No, the challenge of today's pastor is to help the people to get a right idea about God. We are prone to speak platitudes about God; we discover some Hebrew and Greek words and use them or their translation. So we can use terms like Yahweh, Elohim, El Shaddai, Adonai and we've learned to say God is omnipotent, omniscient, omnipresent, and more. If all we have is a superficial or emotional relationship with or knowledge about God, the question that is haunting us in this scientific age is: 'what is our idea of God?' When we've done with the platitudes and the strange words, and waving our hands in the air, when we've come down from the stratosphere, off the ceiling, the question our children and grandchildren are asking is pastor, overseer, mother, father, who or what is God? No religion can rise higher than its idea of God. No church can rise higher than its idea of God. Our praying, our worship, our giving, our living is determined by the idea we have in our heads and in our hearts of God. We are shallow or profound based on our idea of God. Bishop Paul, your task sir above everything else I suggest is to help us to know the God of Abraham, Isaac, Jacob, Paul and indeed the God of Jesus: the Father he kept praying and deferring to. Who is this God that inhabits eternity? Who is the I Am that I Am, the Alpha and Omega? How can we discover this Transcendent One by whose "Power at work in us is able to accomplish abundantly far more than all we can ask or imagine" (Ephesians 3.20).

What I am here to say primarily today is that church must help us find God. Church must not get in the way of discovering God. Church must not become so domesticated, so earthy, so preoccupied with its own business, with navel-gazing that it obscures or hinders us from developing our idea of God. Church must help us to lift up our heads, to look up, take off and soar like eagles in pursuit of the Creator and Sustainer of this great universe, and in whose image we are made. I hope that together we are going to go on a voyage of divine discovery.

TEXTS GENESIS 12.1-9 & ST JOHN 4.31-38

Abraham according to the Bible was called by God to 'Go from his country, kindred and his father's house, to a land "I will show you".' God said (as it were), 'Abraham, I want you to exchange the known for the unknown, the familiar for the unfamiliar, the local for the global, the little picture for the big picture.' God promised to bless Abraham, to give him the land of Canaan, to give him children as many as the sand of the seashore or the stars in the sky, and that through him all the families of the earth would be blessed. We know from the story of the life of Abraham that his journey was far from easy or straightforward. Leaving Haran, Abraham and his household eventually arrived in Canaan, passing through Shechem, Moreh, Bethel, the Negev and eventually into Egypt. Abraham was to find that the place God had in mind for him was already populated with the Philistines. God had called him but there were challenges. Abraham didn't get it all right either. He made some mistakes, some bad judgements – sleeping with his maid and getting her pregnant was not his finest moment! And even by the time of his death, Abraham still had not realised God's promise, but died in faith. I wonder what was his idea of God?

In John's gospel Jesus had just engaged in some cross-cultural evangelism. The Samaritan woman has now gone into the city to tell everybody she met, "come and see a man who told me everything I have ever done, surely he must be the Christ, the Messiah." The disciples apparently unaware of the significance of the moment were concerned that Jesus was talking to a mere woman, and a Samaritan woman at that. But they were also concerned for Jesus' well-being: "Rabbi, teacher, eat something". Jesus may well have replied, 'I have food that you know nothing about; I have inner spiritual sustenance you just don't know about.' And what was that food? "To do the will of him that sent me and to complete his work". Jesus was reorientating their thinking. He used an example from agricultural life. They knew that some crops took four months; you prepare the soil, sow the seeds, then wait four months for the crop. Jesus said we don't have four months to wait for this harvest. Indeed we don't need to wait four months for harvest. Amos had prophesied, "the time surely is coming, says the Lord, when the one who ploughs shall overtake the one who reaps, and the trader of grapes the one who sows the seed" (Amos 9.13). So Jesus said, "lift up your head, look around you, see how the fields are ripe for harvesting." The farmer needed to wait the whole cycle, but God was doing a new work, a quick work; the reproduction cycle was to be divinely collapsed so that the preparer, sower, reaper and trader were as one! Jesus said, "I am sending you to reap where you have not laboured; others have laboured and you are entering into their labour." I wonder what was their idea of God after that lesson?

WHAT MIGHT WE SEE WHEN WE LOOK UP?

I believe God is wanting to change our idea about Him. And we do so best through our experience of God. Like Abraham we must walk with God, make our mistakes, fall down, get up and keep hope and faith alive! Like the disciples we must be challenged about our natural thinking. Jesus wants to introduce us to a God who is Creator and Sustainer of the universe. And church must help every babe in Christ to walk this walk of faith.

The church of God does not exist because of us but because of Christ. And it is this Christ who calls us to journey with him, to look out on the field, the world, which urgently needs to be reaped. As we look out on the mission field what do we see? We see political turmoil – from 'Occupy London' questioning national economic morals to the Arab Spring overturning long-established dictatorships. As we look out we see governments all around the world unsure of how to do politics. Some who a few years ago appeared unmovable have been swept away. The world's political institutions have been shaken to their roots; some of our own parliamentarians are in prison. As we look on the fields we see economic crises. Practically every country, including the USA, China, Japan and our own country, is in the middle of an economic maelstrom. Austerity measures, cuts, credit crunch, fat cats have all become everyday economic terms. The consequences of these political and economic challenges mean joblessness, homelessness, desperation, hopelessness, suicides, euthanasia popularised, and more. As we look on the fields we see faith, all faiths, under attack because some feel it has outlived its usefulness in human development. Some who deny God's existence say, 'Science has removed the need for belief in God'. Our young people at university and in the professions especially need our prayers, support and spiritual education. But we sometimes behave as though these challenges have nothing to do with us; so we keep our heads down and keep quoting Scriptures, as Steve Clifford, General Director of the Evangelical Alliance puts it.

CHALLENGES TO SEEING THE BIG PICTURE

The church cannot simply keep itself warm in a world that is falling apart. Where the latest lifestyle survey says 50% in our country deny the existence of God. And among those who have some faith, more than 50% don't practise. Only 14% of the population go to church regularly. As long as you look down, inward, preoccupied with maintaining structures and the status quo, our sacred cows, the world goes to hell. Why? Because some of us like things just as they are. Don't break up my fruitless unproductive routine. We're happy with the rut we're in, the same old same old. Things can change if they want to but we aren't changing. The definition of insanity is doing the same thing over and over and expecting a different result. But we say we trust in God and we believe in 'PUSH' – pray until something happens. I don't see that policy or philosophy anywhere in Scripture. We must pray and minister. Prayer and fasting are action words, but everything depends on your idea about God.

CONCLUSION

Pastor, as we welcome you, the question is, are we prepared to act differently to get different outcomes? Are we willing to look up, up from the small-mindedness and preoccupation with man-made idols and sacred cows? Are we prepared to move on and up from human standards of holiness and righteousness? Up from so-called Church of God standards? Up to where we see a big God who loves us so much he has invested his character in us and is willing and wanting all his children to grow into him? He invites us in our frail humanity to journey with him. If this church provides a home like a city on a hill where God is big, and where people are nurtured and enabled, people will ask their way to Zion and come home in numbers. Today we are challenged to see the big picture of a big church, responding to a big God who has sent us into a big world with big challenges? Your challenge, pastor, is to lead this local church there!

Address at installation of Bishop Paul McCalla as Pastor of COGOP Aberdeen Street, Winson Green, Birmingham

Part 12

DESTINY

CHAPTER 26

Decision determines destiny (Deuteronomy 30.11-20)

INTRODUCTION

The ten verses of Deuteronomy 30.11-20 illustrate well the causal link between the decisions people make and the consequences of those decisions we see in their lives. The stark choice Israel faced was to accept the terms of a covenant with God and live, or reject it and die. The text shows that God was careful to ensure that the contract he was calling Israel to make a decision about was 'not mysterious', not 'far off' (v11), 'not in heaven' and 'not beyond the sea' (v12): it was made plain in accessible language. So, here's God's deal, "I call heaven and earth as witnesses today against you, that I have set before you life and death, blessing and cursing; therefore choose life, that both you and your descendants may live" (Deuteronomy 30.19). That decision which Israel faced in the wilderness land of Moab reminds us of the ones we face in the wilderness of today's contemporary life. As my topic suggests, there is an intrinsic association between decision and destiny. God is reminding us today that the decisions we make, good or bad, have a direct bearing on how we as individuals and as a church end up. We are reminded too, that God calls us to consider our options and choose life over death.

I want to examine in this sermon what we mean by the words 'decision' and 'destiny', and what they mean for us as individuals and as a church.

DECISION

I want to say four things briefly about decision.

First, dictionaries give many meanings for 'decision'. I have chosen three: 'a resolution reached'; 'the act of making up one's mind'; and 'firmness of purpose or character'. This means that a decision is more than an act. It is a process that leads to a decisive conclusion. The Bible sets the tone for this process in Genesis 1 where God says repeatedly, "let us…" We find in these texts a triune God in discourse with Godself; so "let us make man" in verse 26 is followed by "God created man" in verse 27. This is why we speak of 'reaching' or 'arriving' at a decision. Decision is a journey, a process that calls for sober reflection. Now, I am a keen cricket follower, and the best umpires are those who take a moment to arrive at a decision: they ask themselves, was it a legitimate ball? Did the ball pitch outside leg stump? Would it have missed off stump? Was it too high? Was the batsman playing a shot? All of these considerations lead the umpire to a decision as to whether the batsman is 'out' or 'not out'. Time and again the Bible calls upon us to 'consider', i.e. think, ponder, and weigh the evidence. In the Wisdom Literature of Holy Scripture we read, "He who answers a matter before he hears it, it is folly and a shame to him" (Proverbs 18.13). So, a decision is a conclusion reached after a process of consideration of all the evidence. Decision is never about just making a decision, because there is such a thing as a bad decision. Therefore, how we go about deciding is of paramount importance. The Scriptures call us time and again to make a righteous judgment; consider all the relevant facts, remove our own prejudices and preconceptions, act maturely and make decisions that are soaked in righteousness and justice.

Second, on our own as humans we do not make right and just decisions. We do this best when we consciously recognise our working relationship with God. The resources we need to arrive at sound judgments or sound decisions come from the two sources of our existence: the human and the divine. Some Christians seem to think that when a big decision faces us all we have to do is fast and pray; that is, they spiritualise the matter entirely. Good as fasting and prayer are, we must not forget our human side of reasoning and our emotional and psychological feelings. Such are the spiritual foes, principalities and powers arrayed against us, that it is not enough to base our decisions on the notion that we have fasted and prayed. The Bible tells us to try the spirit, and use our spiritual judgment. Too many of us believe that the human mind, our power to reason, is not of God, so we eschew our minds, and embrace our feelings. The Christian mind is a renewed mind (Romans 12.1-2) and so if there is anybody on earth who ought to have sound thinking, sound reasoning as a trait, it surely should be the people of God. I contend that the path to good decision making is when we combine the human and divine, using the faculties God has given us even as we recognise our limitations in deference to the all knowing God through prayer. The writer of Proverbs 3.5-6 says, "Trust in the Lord with all your heart, and lean not on your own understanding; in all your ways acknowledge him, and he shall direct your paths". God wants to work with us in all our decision-making.

Third, as humans when we make a decision we may know some of the facts, some of the benefits and some of the downside. But, we can never know the whole picture. So our human/divine relationship gives us faith to believe that even though we don't know everything, God who does will make up for our lack. Our faith does not give us license to take shortcuts; it doesn't make our decision-making easier, but it gives the believer assurance that after we have done our best, God does the rest. As ever, our faith in God acts as an anchor for the soul; it under-girds our belief that decisions are best reached when we call upon both our human and divine resources, since as the Apostle Paul puts it, we are labourers together with God.

Fourth, a decision means more than words. For a decision to be effective it has to be accompanied by thought out action. God, in saying, "let us make man", took dust, formed man and breathed into him the breath of life. Whatever your decision is about, action must follow to bring it to pass. You can decide to live in a castle but to actually live in a castle you will need to pursue a set of actions that culminate in your getting a castle to buy or rent. Simply deciding to live in one doesn't make it so. If you are serious about your decision to get a degree you must find a university, sign on, turn up to classes, study hard, and stay the course. Anything else is wishful thinking. Words are cheap, action put flesh on the bone of our decision. So, a decision is the conclusion reached at the end of a process of reasoning that is backed by action to get things done.

DESTINY

Destiny has been described as, "The pre-determined or inevitable course of events". Destiny can also be viewed as the ultimate end or purpose for which a thing or person was made. All of this can sound like a *fait accompli* – like destiny is something that happens to you with you having no say at all. If you believe you are born to a destiny that is beyond your control, then you might be right to throw your hands up in the air and say, 'Que sera sera, whatever will be will be'. Allow me to make two key points about destiny.

First, it isn't really possible to speak of destiny without pausing to refer to the hugely problematic theological area of what's called variously election, foreordination or predestination. From at least the time of Augustine of Hippo in the 5th century to Reformers like John Calvin and Martin Luther in the 16th century, theologians have wrestled with the point at which God's sovereignty meets human will. Excuse me if I don't attempt to resolve this age-old theological dilemma in this presentation. But I do need to say a few words about it. I believe as the reformers believed that salvation is by grace and does not depend on human merit or virtue. However, I find it difficult to accept the Augustinian and Calvinist view that God has predestined those who will be saved and, therefore, condemned to hell those he did not predestinate. I find Karl Barth's argument persuasive that it is in Jesus we find our predestination to salvation or damnation. As the Bible says, "for God so loved the world that he gave his only begotten Son, that whosoever believes in him has everlasting life" (St John 3.16). So, everyone who chooses Jesus inherits that which is predestinated in him – eternal life. Those who reject life receive the predestination of rejection: death.

There are some things that God has foreordained that are not open to human will. He has set the framework within which the cosmos exists; he has predetermined the fulfilment of life as we know it. But within the grand plan of God, life is very much what we make it. We know for example that God gives us gifts and talents, but the fulfilment of those talents depend upon our willingness to work hard and dedicate ourselves to their development, seeking opportunities to apply them. You may be a talented preacher but if you do not spend time in preparation you will never fulfil your destiny as a preacher. In an excellent book by American writer Malcolm Gladwell titled 'Outliers' he insists that it takes 10,000 hours for anybody, from the Beatles to Bill Gates, to become world class at anything. What you do with what you have determines what happens to what you have. Your destiny is in your hands. The symbiotic human/divine relationship demands that as God does his part, we do ours. It's up to each of us whether we trade on our talents, develop them or bury them in the ground. Our attitude determines whether we are profitable or unprofitable stewards. Your destiny in this life – materially and spiritually – depend on the decisions you make. The sky is the limit with God.

One of the things I admire President Obama most for, is his way of making decisions. Last year, after the US General in Afghanistan requested 30,000 more troops to execute the war against the Taliban, the President took over three months to consider the request. Why? Because the destiny of the war and (he would argue) the security of the American people depended on the decision. So the President commissioned reports, consulted with colleagues, listened to opposing voices, consulted with allies abroad and eventually agreed to the request. You see it's not enough to make a decision; it is important to make the right decision because the quality of your destiny depends on it. You see, destiny is not always a positive word. A person who makes a decision to steal or murder will go into the destiny that is determined by that decision and action: it may be community service, a custodial sentence or in some parts of the world limb amputation or even execution. Every decision leads to a destiny and this is why we must strive to gather all the evidence, use our wisdom and seek divine guidance in arriving at our decisions. Finally, I want to look at the link between decision and destiny on a personal and corporate level.

First, decision and destiny on the personal level. There are at least two types of decisions we have to make. Those decisions posed by external forces and those posed by ourselves. From either source, it is not easy to make decisions, especially big ones. This is why so many of us put them off, or make rash ones. Each of us must take responsibility for the decisions that are ours to make and if we have a methodology for decision-making then we are likely to find it easier to make good decisions. For example here is a seven-point decision-making process: i) examine the issue carefully from all sides; ii) seek advice from those who may be favourable; iii) seek the views of those who may be unfavourable; iv) commit it to active prayer and reflection; v) gather together all the known facts and views; vi) make a decision; vii) stick by your decision. When a child of God engages in a process like this, you do so aware that God is watching your back because we are in partnership with him. He who has foreordained us to partake in the glory of his Son is interested in our affairs; he wants us to do well. Our Shalom, peace and prosperity, gives glory to God. God doesn't want us to stop at the crossroads in our lives endlessly marking time, frustrated. No, he wants us to actively engage in pursuing our God-given destiny and that means making sound decisions about the matters that arise along the way. Some of us have been at some crossroads for far too long, fearful of making a decision. Well, if you don't make it, it will make you because you will be eventually overrun by events.

As I've been suggesting, personal decision-making is inextricably linked to personal destiny. And remember that your destiny is in your hands to shape. Looking at what God has given to you in terms of gifts, abilities, favour and grace, you can see through spiritual eyes where you can go with God. Joseph through his dreams realised what his destiny was and made decisions that facilitated that destiny. So when Mrs Potiphar said, "lie with me", Joseph instinctively knew that that would compromise his destiny. Often we don't dream enough; we don't envision enough; we don't blue-sky think enough. We serve a great big wonderful God and yet we are often guilty of small thinking which is a telltale sign of mediocre destiny ambition. If you thought that you had it within you to be a millionaire and set that as your destiny, you would judge requests for your time against that destination. If you took seriously that God has called you to preach you must begin to prepare yourself through study and consistent moral living. If you decide to marry and have a good life of mutual fulfilment then you must deal with unwanted advances from others in that light. If you decide that you want to retire to the Caribbean in ten years time, you make decisions consistent with that personal destiny. However, if you have no plans, the devil finds work for idle hands. 'Idle donkey follow cane bump go a pound', meaning every little puny suggestion people bring to you, you are inclined to say yes, because you have nothing better to do.

Each child of God needs to spend time understanding their destiny. God knows the plans he has for you, but do you? The Bible asks who knows the mind of Christ and responds that we have the mind of Christ. Get into God and discover His plans for you. Although I didn't see the full picture, some years ago I saw myself working in the field of ecumenism so I applied for a job in the field and was appointed director of the Centre for Black and White Christian Partnership. Some years ago I imagined that I could achieve a PhD by studying for it! I set myself a target of getting there by the time I reached 50, and with help from my wife, family and friends, with lots of burning the midnight oil, after 8 years of part-time study at Sheffield University I achieved it. There were many hurdles to climb but I had an aim, a goal, a destiny in mind. Over thirty-five years ago I decided I wanted to spend the rest of my life with Novelette as my wife and we are still together. There have been hurdles to climb, but I have a destination in mind. Many years ago I decided to follow Jesus believing this leads to peace with God now and after death; I'm still walking. You must have a goal, a destiny, and when you have you deal with what life throws at you in the spirit of your destiny.

Second, decision and destiny on a corporate level. In the same way that we are faced with decisions that determine our personal destiny, so too do our churches, local, national and international. The decisions we make corporately follow the same pattern as personal decision-making. The church has decisions to make that are the result of external factors and it has decisions as a result of its internal situation. Sad to say, when it comes to decision-making, truth is many churches are not thinking churches; they just go through the motions as though the God we serve is an unthinking God. So often we do not pose appropriate questions internally; deliberations are about things of little consequence, and when we face decisions we spiritualise them. Like the individual faced with decisions, the church could do with adopting the same seven point plan I mentioned earlier: i) examine the issue carefully from all sides; ii) seek advice from those who may be favourable; iii) seek the views of those who may be unfavourable; iv) commit it to active prayer and reflection; v) gather together all the known facts and views; vi) make a decision; vii) stick by your decision.

But if our corporate decision-making process is flawed, it's either because we are unclear about our corporate destiny or we embrace a mediocre concept of our corporate destiny. We know the ultimate destiny of the catholic church; the 'bride' of Christ is the consumption of all things in Christ. But what we don't know is the potential of a local church or a denomination. That is left to the ambition, gifts and talents of that church and in the end our destiny is what we make it. When you understand that your destiny is in your own hands as a local church or as a denomination, you will spend time pondering your destiny as a church, decide where you want to be, and make plans that you then execute to get where you dream about. The decisions we make or don't make indicate our understanding of our destiny and determine our destiny.

So in conclusion, we embrace a destiny befitting our privileged position as the children of God, individually and corporately. Whether the challenges come from within or without, we make decisions in keeping with our big destiny. We may kid ourselves, but as with Israel, the sources for our decision are not mysterious, not far off, not in heaven, not beyond the sea. In answering the question, 'why am I here?' we must move in our destiny, make sound decisions and stick by them as we head towards personal and corporate fulfilment. And we are assured that as we do so with all our human energies, God the transcendent One is with us. Amen!

Sermon preached at a local church in England

Part 13

PARENTING

CHAPTER 27

It's all in the parenting – stupid!

Guns, drugs, knives… it's easy to look to schools or the government for answers to the problems faced, or caused, by our young people. I argue that the way forward lies in the values taught at home.

The headlines just keep coming: "Anti-gun campaigners demand ban on 50 Cent video game" (The Voice, 1 December 2005); "Where life is guns, gangs and violence" (The Telegraph, 16 February 2007); "Boy, 16, shot dead in gang gun battle" (The Guardian, 19 October 2007). And while many of us are keen to stress that this is not exclusively a 'Black' problem, but an urban one, the reality is that a disproportionate number of Black and other ethnic minorities live in this country's urban areas, and so it is impossible to speak about urban issues without referring to the Black people who live there.

Lee Jasper, former advisor to London's mayor on equality issues, pointed out recently that Black people are five times more likely to be jailed than Whites; Black boys are 2.6 times more likely to be a victim of violent crime, 1.6 times more likely to be a robbery victim, and 5.5 times more likely to be murdered than their White counterpart. Unfortunately some of these statistics are brought about by what has been called 'Black on Black' violence. I do not believe Black boys shoot or knife other Blacks because they are Black; they do so within the contested space of their urban existence and the real experience of deprivation, lack of opportunities, poor housing, poor education and lack of facilities.

However, poverty has never been a good excuse for bad behaviour. Many people of my generation, who grew up in the 1960s and 1970s, especially if they started life in the Caribbean, Africa or Asia, know at first hand the social challenges of poverty. Yet, we were taught to embrace faith in God, to love life as something sacred, to respect our elders, and to have what people used to call 'manners'. In fact, growing up in Jamaica, I often heard the phrase, 'Boy, good manners will take you through this world.'

Today, there is a palpable fear of the young. This has replaced the historic poly-parenting I grew up with, where the maxim, 'it takes a whole village to raise a child' meant something. Recently I described the phenomenon of gangs that blight our cities through the use of drugs, guns and knives as 'socialising gone wrong'. There is absolutely nothing wrong with young people clustering in social groups by area, family, school, church and other social definers. What we can and should do is create the environment where such clustering is healthy by being multi-dimensional, productive and contributing to the well-being and development of individuals and the wider community.

Although we welcome the policies and initiatives from national and local government and other statutory agencies that seek to tackle social deprivation and underachievement in education, training and employment, whatever we do 'out there' can never match what we do 'in here' in terms of lasting effectiveness. Again, if I return to my Jamaican upbringing, I learnt young that, 'You have fi learn fi dance a yaad before you dance abraad.' In other words, the basis of the moral and character training needed to take us successfully through life begins at home, not in government schemes.

The Bible is quite right when it says, "train up a child in the way he should go, and when he is old he will not depart from it" (Proverbs 22:6). What we learn at home as youngsters will always remain seminal to our understanding of self, other and the world. As good as church and school are as centres of learning and training, their influence rank lower than the home in lasting influence.

So, I am calling for compulsory parenting classes for every pregnant woman and expectant father during the antenatal phase. After which postnatal health checks should go hand in hand with instruction and information about good parenting. The sooner we stop blaming society and recognise that life and training begin at home, the sooner we crack the phenomenon of youth gangs blighting our corporate life.

First published by Conservative Christian Fellowship 22 January, 2008

SELECT BIBLIOGRAPHY

Aldred, J.D., *A Black Majority Church's Future*, unpublished Thesis, University of Sheffield, 1994

Aldred, Joe, *Preaching with Power: Sermons by Black Preachers*, Cassall, 1998

Aldred, Joe, *Respect – understanding Caribbean British Christianity*, Epworth, 2005

Aldred, Joe, (ed), *Sisters with Power*, London: Continuum, 2000

Aldred, Joe & Ogbo, Keno eds., *The Black Church in the 21st Century*, Epworth, 2010

Alibhai-Brown, Yasmin, W*ho do we think we are?* Penguin Books, 2000

Anderson, Allan, *An Introduction to Pentecostalism*, Cambridge University Press, 2004

Anderson, Victor, *Beyond Ontological Blackness*, Continuum, 1999

Arnold, Selwyn, *From Scepticism to Hope*, Grove Books, 1992

Barton, Mukti, *Rejection, Resistance and Resurrection*, Darton Longman and Todd, 2005

Beckford, R, *Dread and Pentecostal*, SPCK, 2000

Beckford, Robert, *God of the Rahtid,* Darton Longman & Todd, 2001

Bragg, Lord Melvyn, *The Book of Books: The Radical Impact of the King James Bible 1611-2011*, Hodder & Stoughton, 2011

Bruggemann, Walter, *Texts Under Negotiation: Bible and Postmodern Imagination,* Augsburg Fortress, 1993

Campbell, Gordon, *Bible: The Story of the King James Version*, OUP Oxford, 2010

Cantuar, Bishop George, *Foreword - The Passing Winter*, Church Publishing House, 1996.

Cathcart, Brian, *The Case of Stephen Lawrence*, Penguin Books, 1999

Catholic Association for Racial Justice, *Racism in British Society*, 1993

Clarke, Adam, *The Bethany Parallel Commentary*, Minnesota: Bethany House Publishers, 1983

Cone, James, *Black Theology and Black Power*, Harper and Row, 1969

Copley, Terence, *The Bible: The Story of the Book,* Bible Society, 1990

Davies, Brian, (ed), *Philosophy of Religion*, Cassell, 2000

Drane, John, *Cultural Change and Biblical Faith*, Paternoster, 2000

Edwards, Joel, (ed) in, *Let's Praise Him Again*, Kingsway Publications, 1992

Faus, Jose Ignacio Gonzalez, '*Sin*' in Jon Sobrino & Ignacio Ellacuria (eds), Systematic Theology, SCM Press, 1996
Felder, C. Hope, *Troubling Biblical Waters,* Maryknoll, NY, Orbis Books, 1989
Gerloff, R.I.H., *A Plea for British Black Theologies,* Frankfurt am Main, Peter Lang, 1992
Gilroy, Paul, *Against Race*, The Belknap Press, 2000
Gladwell, Malcolm, *Outliers: The Story of Success*, Penguin, 2009
Glass, John, *Building Bigger People*, Authentic, 2008
Grant, Paul & Patel, Raj, (eds), *A Time to Speak*, Birmingham Black Theology Working Group, 1990
Grudem, Wayne, *Tyndale New Testament Commentaries*, Leicester: Inter-Varsity Press, 1988
Gutierrez, Gustavo, *The Power of the Poor in History*, London: SCM Press, 1983
Hannaford, Ivan, *Race: The History of and Idea in the West*, Baltimore, Maryland, 1996
Jagessar, Michael & Reddie, Anthony, (eds), *Postcolonial Black British Theology*, Peterborough: Epworth, 2007
Lartey, Emmanuel, (ed), *Black theology in Britain, issue 1*, 1998
Marshall, I. Howard, *Acts: Tyndale New Testament Commentaries*, Grand Rapids, Michigan: Inter Varcity Press, 1980
Martin, Larry, *The life and ministry of William J Seymour*, Christian Life Books, 1999
McGrath, Alistair, *Christian Theology,* Blackwell Publishers, Johns Hopkins University Press, 1996
Moore, N., *Pulpit Confessions*, BSB Publishing Co., 1998
Parekh, Bhikhu, *Rethinking Multiculturalism*, Palgrave, 2000
Anthony, Reddie, (ed), *Black Theology – an International Journal*, Equinox, Volume 4 Number 2, 2006
Reddie, Richard, *Abolition*, Lion Hudson, 2007
Sewell, Tony, *Generating Genius: Black Boys in Love, Ritual and Schooling,* Trentham Books, 2009
Silva, Moises, *Has the Church Misread the Bible? Vol. 1: Foundations of Contemporary Interpretation,* Academic Books, 1987
Smith, Io, *An Ebony Cross*, Marshall Morgan and Scott, 1989
Sturge, Mark, *Look what the Lord has Done,* Scripture Union, 2005
Walker, Robin, *When We Ruled*, Every Generation Media, 2006
Wilkinson, John L., *Church in Black and White,* Saint Andrew Press, 1993
Wilmore, Gayraud, *Black Religion and Black Radicalism*, New York: Orbis, 1998